BRANCH LINES TO EAST GRINSTEAD

Vic Mitchell and Keith Smith

Other Middleton Press albums to feature stations included in this volume are -

Branch Lines to Tunbridge Wells contains Groombridge, Tunbridge Wells West, Oxted, Hurst Green and Lewes.

East Croydon to Three Bridges and *Three Bridges to Brighton* have many other views of Three Bridges station.

Haywards Heath to Seaford features the Ardingly - Horsted Keynes route and also Lewes.

Brighton to Eastbourne includes other views and maps of Lewes.

Croydon to East Grinstead has a fresh look at Oxted and stations south thereof and includes the recent developments.

Cover photograph:
A 2-6-4 tank at the head of the up train on 30th April 1955. Southern crews refused to accept the official BR power classification of 4P and painted P4 on the platform when needing a mark by which to stop the locomotive to ensure that it was level with the water crane. (R.C.Riley)

Published 1984
First reprint 1985
Second reprint 1990
Third reprint 1995
Fourth reprint July 2000

ISBN 0 906520 07 X

Published by
Middleton Press
Easebourne Lane
Midhurst, West Sussex
GU29 9AZ
Tel: 01730 813169
Fax: 01730 812601

Printed & bound by Biddles Ltd,
Guildford and Kings Lynn

INDEX TO SECTIONS

INDEX TO STATIONS

MAPS

Except where otherwise stated, the scale is 25″ to 1 mile but the following initial letters apply throughout.

BM Bench Mark
Cr Crane
MP Mile Post
SB Signal Box
SP Signal Post

ACKNOWLEDGEMENTS

We would like to record our appreciation of the help received from everyone named in the credits to the captions and also from the following: R. Harmer, C. Hayward, R.A. Holder, M.J. Leppard, J. Minnis, D. Osborne, Mrs. E. Wallis, D. Wallis and M. Welch. We are grateful to G. Croughton and N. Langridge for the use of tickets from their collections and to M. Chevis, D. Dornom, C. Gibbins, M.J. Grainger and D. Mercer for photographic assistance. We are again thankful for the valuable criticism and support given by Mrs. E. Fisk, N. Stanyon and, not least, our patient wives.

GEOGRAPHICAL SETTING

East Grinstead was in the county of East Sussex until 1974, when it was transferred to West Sussex. It lies about 400 feet above sea level, supported by the central Weald sandstone mass of the Hastings Beds. These hills are divided by the incisions of a number of infant rivers radiating in all directions and also carry the railway lines linking Three Bridges with Tunbridge Wells and Newick with Lingfield. North of the latter the route crosses the relatively flat Wealden clay (good for brickmaking) and the River Eden before reaching Oxted, situated on the attractive sandy hills of the Hythe Beds, within sight of the chalk of the North Downs. The line from the south starts from Lewes, where the station site is partly dug into the chalk of the South Downs, close to the Ouse Gap. After following the River Ouse for three miles the line traverses similar geology, and therefore scenery, as described south of Oxted, but in the reverse order.

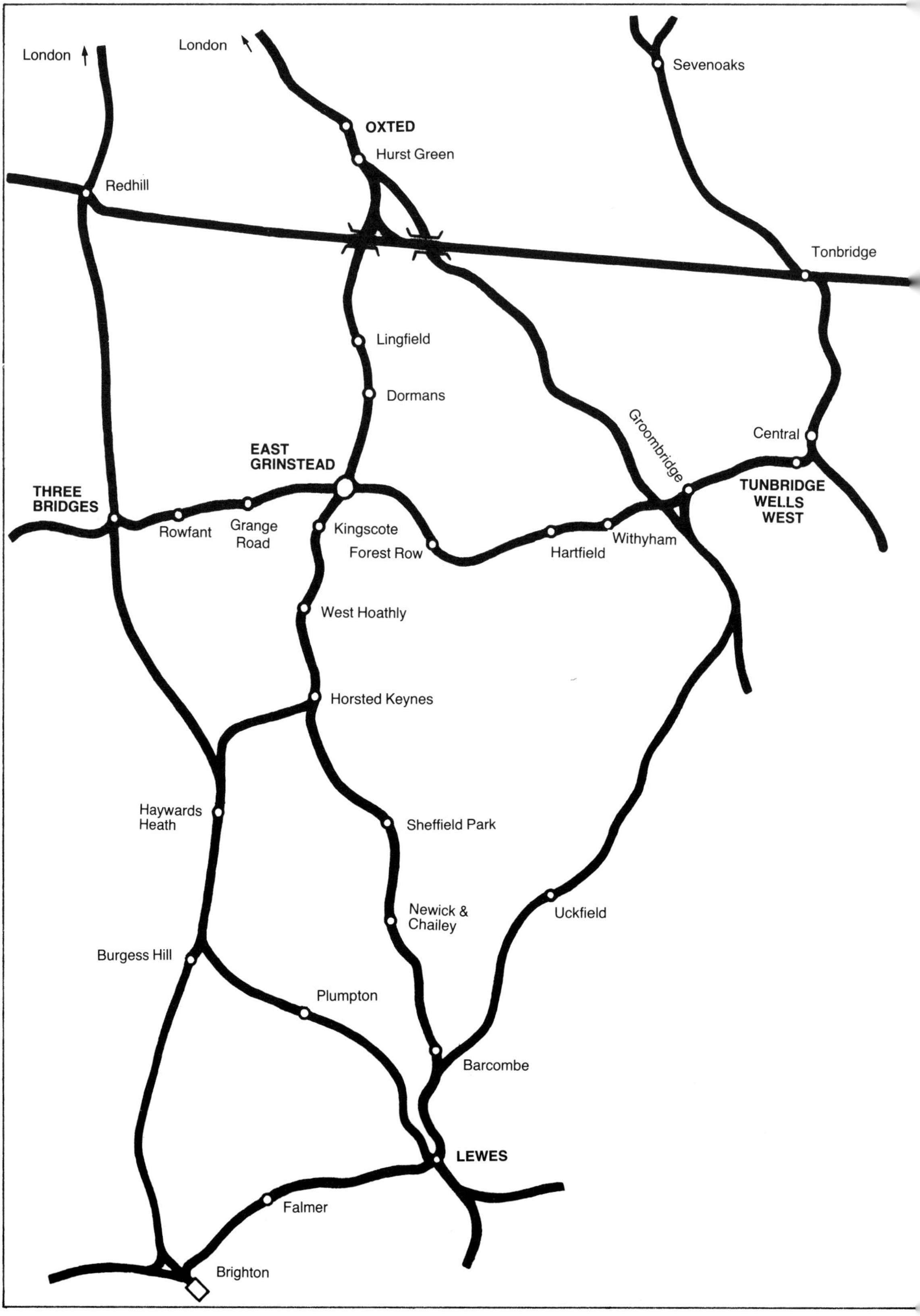
London
London
Sevenoaks
OXTED
Hurst Green
Redhill
Tonbridge
Lingfield
Dormans
Groombridge
Central
EAST GRINSTEAD
THREE BRIDGES
TUNBRIDGE WELLS WEST
Rowfant
Grange Road
Kingscote
Forest Row
Hartfield
Withyham
West Hoathly
Horsted Keynes
Haywards Heath
Sheffield Park
Newick & Chailey
Uckfield
Burgess Hill
Plumpton
Barcombe
LEWES
Falmer
Brighton

HISTORICAL BACKGROUND

The first branch line to East Grinstead sprouted from the London Brighton & South Coast Railway's main line at Three Bridges. The East Grinstead Railway Co. was formed by local businessmen and the customary *First Sod Ceremony* took place on 22nd November 1853. The line was opened on 9th July 1855, with one intermediate station at Rowfant and it was operated by the LBSCR, who eventually acquired it.

The second branch was a continuation of the first and resulted from the formation of another company by local enterprise – The East Grinstead, Groombridge and Tunbridge Wells Railway Company. First sods were cut on 18th July 1863 and again the LBSCR arranged to operate the line. Failure to comply with official requirements delayed the opening *four times* and when it did eventually happen, on 1st October 1866, the local press was so tired of waiting they failed to report it!

The third branch was from the south. Authority was given to the Lewes and East Grinstead Railway Co. to construct a line north from Culver Junction, on the Lewes to Tunbridge Wells direct route. Unlike the first two branches, provision was made for double track in the civil engineering, but there was never more than single track laid south of Horsted Keynes. Station facilities were lavish, costing a massive £17,000 each, and in 17 miles no less than eleven signal boxes were provided by the LBSCR for the opening on 1st August 1882.

The fourth line to this Sussex crossroads was from the north. After a start over 20 years earlier, the Croydon, Oxted and East Grinstead Railway was opened on 10th March 1884. An agreement between the South Eastern Railway and the LBSCR in 1848 gave the former the rights to the territory to the north-east of Redhill. For the LBSCR to operate the new line it had to be a joint line from South Croydon to the point where it crossed the former SER main line from Redhill to Tonbridge at Crowhurst Junction, where a connecting spur was provided. A connecting spur was also laid at East Grinstead to link with the Tunbridge Wells line. Double track was used throughout, including the spurs.

The formation of the Southern Railway in 1923 had little effect on these lines. Residents of Tunbridge Wells however found that at last their two stations now had different names, receiving the suffixes *Central* (ex SECR) and *West* (ex LBSCR). The proposed electrification from Croydon to Haywards Heath via Oxted, East Grinstead and Horsted Keynes never came to fruition.

The transition to British Railways in 1948 also had no immediate effect. However, whilst BR planned to close the East Grinstead to Lewes service on 13th June 1955, the last train rites had to be enacted on 28th May due to an impending strike. They did not reckon on Miss Bessemer of Chailey discovering that under the original Act of Parliament the closure could only be effected by Government authority and not by the railway alone. They were therefore obliged to reinstate a service (4 trains a day demanded by the Act) on 7th August 1956. Deliberate lack of through booking facilities was one of the reasons that such terms as *spite service* or *sulky service* came into use. The end finally came on 16th March 1958. All was not lost, for in December 1959 the Bluebell Railway Preservation Society gained control of most of the line between Horsted Keynes and Sheffield Park and has recently had its sights set on northward extension.

The west to east service between Three Bridges and Tunbridge Wells West last operated on 1st January 1967, leaving East Grinstead, home town of Dr. Beeching, where it started its railway history, at the end of a single branch.

←

Map showing the area covered by this album, the limits being the towns shown in capital letters. (I. Harden)

ACCIDENTS

1868 was notable for two unusual incidents, both involving bulls. On 21st June, Craven 0-4-2 ST no.167 was hauling a cattle train near Hartfield when the driver was warned of a runaway bull on the line. Whilst proceeding with caution, the axle of a cattle truck containing cows broke, causing a derailment. The bull, attracted by the noise of females in distress, descended upon the train at such speed that the driver broke his collar bone whilst racing for the refuge of his footplate. The bull was recaptured with the aid of one cow as a bait. On 2nd July, three boys derailed a 2–2–2 locomotive (no.7, built by Bodmer) at Groombridge by jamming stones in the points. The guard gave chase, but one of the boys ran off into a field where he was severely gored by a bull.

On 5th January 1883, a D class tank no. 273 *Dornden* ran into a rock fall near High Rocks whilst hauling eight coaches, all of which were fortunately empty. The same locomotive was involved in a notable incident on December 14th of the following year. Major Edwards, a wealthy landowner at Groombridge, had difficulty in boarding the last train home from Heathfield owing to extreme intoxication. The train was again delayed by him at Mayfield due to a prolonged visit to the Gents, after which the guard decided to lock him into a compartment. Whilst speeding north the Major surprised the locomotive crew by appearing on the footplate, complaining that a dog had chased him through the window and along the outside of the train. The fireman obligingly despatched the dog with his shovel after which the driver settled the unwelcome visitor onto some coats laid on the floor. On arrival at Groombridge, they were unable to wake or move him and so proceeded to Tunbridge Wells. Whilst standing at signals outside the station, the Major awoke, announced "Groombridge, Groombridge, all change," leapt from the footplate, fell down an embankment and disappeared without trace into a flooded stream. Whilst the reports were being given at the station, a distressed young booking clerk burst into the room complaining that a wet tramp, pestered by an invisible dog, was demanding a ticket to Groombridge after the last train had left. A special was arranged and the staff eventually fined for incompetence, but the Major discreetly sent a cheque for £25.

At Newick and Chailey station on 4th January 1883, a down train started away against the signals and was derailed in the refuge siding.

Having missed the last train to his home at Withyham from Tunbridge Wells, a drunken soldier, who had formerly been a locomotive fireman, made off in an unattended EI tank engine (no. 107 *Alderney*) on Christmas Eve 1893. He travelled *up* the *down* line blowing the whistle irregularly! The noise attracted the attention of the driver of a train about to leave Groombridge on a collision course.

Bradshaw 1869

WALTERS' RAILWAY CONVENIENCE

FOR

GENTLEMEN, LADIES, INVALIDS, AND CHILDREN.

This Convenience can be worn imperceptibly with the greatest comfort and security.

WALTERS' HUNTING BELTS AND SUSPENDERS OF ALL DESCRIPTIONS.

MANUFACTURER OF TRUSSES AND ENEMA SYRINGES.

ELASTIC STOCKINGS to lace and to draw on.

WALTERS' ELASTIC BELTS, for Ladies during Pregnancy and after Accouchement.

F. Walters has received highly satisfactory Testimonials to the efficiency of his Belts, which are recommended by the most eminent Professional Men in England.

FREDERICK WALTERS,

16, MOORGATE STREET, BANK, E.C.

N.B.—Entrance at Private Door. A Lady in attendance.
French and German spoken.

He advised the signalman who diverted the drunken driver into a siding, from where he ran off across the fields with Porter Evans and the station master's dog in pursuit. The local constable was summoned but in his excitement he fell off his bicycle into a ditch, where he lay unconscious all night. In the meantime the soldier had been locked up in the station oil store, guarded by Evans and the dog, until handed over to a relief constable on Christmas Day.

There was more excitement on the line many years later, in 1942, when a Brighton to Oxted train was shot-up by a German aircraft. The train had just left Barcombe and so the driver stopped it in the shelter of Cinder Hill Tunnel, which was only 63 yards long!

Disaster was again averted on 3rd March 1954 when an engineer's train ran out of control through Forest Row, became derailed and pulled the signal wire which invited the 8.37 p.m. from Tunbridge Wells West to collide with the wreckage. Smart work by the station master with a red lamp stopped this happening (see photo no. 101).

On 29th July 1955 an engine collided with some coaches at East Grinstead High Level but no injuries or derailment occurred.

Whilst shunting the 5.20 a.m. goods train from Three Bridges at Rowfant on 15th Jauuary 1957, a standard class 4 tank no. 42068 ran through the end of a siding, owing to a misunderstanding, but little damage was caused.

We have found no record of injury to passengers whilst travelling on the branch lines to East Grinstead and are pleased to publish this good news.

TRAIN SERVICES

The first branch to East Grinstead, upon opening, was provided with six trains each way on weekdays and two on Sundays. This was increased to as many as nine and three respectively over the ensuing years and changed little when the line was extended to Tunbridge Wells. In 1881, a through train from London, non-stop between Three Bridges and East Grinstead, was tried. More successful was the slip coach, which was shed at speed from a south coast express before it reached Three Bridges and then hauled by a branch line engine as far as Forest Row. This service operated from 1888 until the main line was electrified in 1932. By 1955, the line west from East Grinstead had the luxury of 17 weekday and 10 Sunday return journeys. Diesel-electric sets started running in 1962 and the last steam trains operated in June 1965, at the same time as the 24-hour clock was introduced into the timetables.

The line from Lewes had four weekday trains in its first year but no Sunday service. When the route was extended northwards from East Grinstead this was increased to six, with an additional four to and from Brighton via Haywards Heath, and two journeys on Sundays. An infrequent service, with some trains running through to Brighton and/or London, was provided throughout the life of this line.

The line from Oxted initially had four return trips per day and this was later supplemented by trains taking more direct routes between London and Tunbridge Wells either via Edenbridge Town or turning off at Crowhurst Junction to travel via Tonbridge.

Of the many special trains run during the last 100 years of railway activity at Oxted, one must be mentioned. It was in the 1880s and was a sixteen-coach trial trip to Tunbridge Wells hauled by a massive 0–6–6–0 Fairlie

Bradshaw 1890

THREE BRIDGES, EAST GRINSTEAD, and TUNBRIDGE WELLS.—London, Brighton, and South Coast.

Miles from Three Bdgs	Down.	Week Days. mrn	mrn	mrn	mrn	mrn	aft	aft	aft	aft	aft	aft		Sndys mrn	aft
	Victoria 72..dep	....	....	7 35	10 5	1140	1 30	2 3	4 0	....	5 52	7 8	....	8 20	6 30
	72 London Bridge "	5 45	....	7 50	9 45	12 0	....	2 5	4 5	5 5	....	7 20	....	8 30	6 40
	Three Bridges..dep	7 10	....	9 10	1118	1 5	2 35	3 30	5 8	5 52	....	8 30	....	9 30	8 25
2¼	Rowfant	7 15	....	9 15	1123	1 10	2 40	3 35	5 13	5 57	....	8 35	....	9 35	8 30
4	Grange Road	7 20	....	9 21	1128	1 15	2 45	3 40	5 18	6 2	....	8 40	....	9 40	8 35
6¾	East Grinstead ar	7 30	....	9 29	1138	1 25	2 54	3 50	5 27	6 12	....	8 50	....	9 50	8 45
	(High Level) dp		8 17	9 36	....	1 28	2 55	4 4	5 29	....	6 53	8 58	....	9 58	8 47
10	Forest Row *	....	8 24	9 43	....	1 35	3 2	4 11	5 37	....	6 59	9 5	....	10 5	8 54
12¼	Hartfield	....	8 32	9 51	....	1 43	3 10	Sats only.	5 45	....	a	9 13	....	1013	9 2
14¼	Withyham	....	8 36	9 55	....	1 46	3 14		5 49	....	....	9 17	....	1017	9 6
17¾	Groombridge 66, 77	....	8 42	10 1	....	1 51	3 18		5 54	....	7 11	9 22	....	1022	9 11
20¾	Tunbridge Wells 90	....	8 50	1010	....	2 2	3 26		6 2	....	7 18	9 31	....	1030	9 19

Miles.	Up.	Week Days. mrn	mrn	mrn	mrn	mrn	mrn	aft	aft	aft		Sndys mrn	aft
	Tunbridge Wells dp	....	7 25	9 0	10 0	....	1125	2 20	3 32	6 15	....	7 15	5 55
3	Groombridge	....	7 31	9 6	10 6	....	1131	2 26	3 38	6 21	....	7 21	6 1
5¾	Withyham	....	7 38	9 12	b	....	1136	2 31	3 43	6 26	....	7 26	6 6
6¾	Hartfield	....	7 43	9 17	....	....	1140	2 35	3 47	6 30	....	7 30	6 10
10¾	Forest Row *	....	7 51	9 25	1017	....	1148	2 43	3 54	6 38	....	7 38	6 18
13¾	East Grinstead ar	....	8 0	9 34	1026	....	1157	2 52	4 3	6 47	....	7 47	6 27
	(High Level) dp	6 40	8 7	9 36	....	1145	1159	2 55	4 6	6 53	....	7 49	6 29
16½	Grange Road	6 46	8 16	9 43	....	1151	12 5	3 1	4 12	6 59	....	7 55	6 35
17¾	Rowfant ....[68 72	6 51	8 21	9 48	....	1156	1210	3 6	4 17	7 4	....	8 0	6 40
20¾	Three Bridges 74,	6 58	8 29	9 56	....	12 4	1217	3 14	4 24	7 12	....	8 8	6 48
49¾	74 London Bdge.arr	8 17	9 45	1048	1125	....	1 17	4 20	5 48	8 33	....	1027	8 15
49¾	Victoria 74.. "	8 27	10 5	11 0	1125	....	1 44	4 27	5 43	....	....	1056	8 16

locomotive, awaiting export to Mexico. This was of the double-ended type familiar today on the Festiniog Railway.

BR introduced a new timetable for the area in June 1955, which David Gould described as "a work of utter brillance". It consisted basically of a regular hourly service between Victoria and Tunbridge Wells West by way of Oxted and East Grinstead, with motor train connections at these two places to Tunbridge Wells West via Edenbridge Town and Three Bridges respectively.

From 1967, when East Grinstead once again became the terminus of a branch line, an hourly service was provided seven days a week by DEMUs. A similar hourly service was operated between Tonbridge and Eridge, serving two of the stations included in this album, Tunbridge Wells West and Groombridge, but this line closed on 7th July 1985.

Electrification of London - East Grinstead services on 5th October 1987 brought a 30-minute interval timetable, although trains were still hourly in the evenings and on Sundays.

LONDON, EAST GRINSTEAD, and TUNBRIDGE WELLS.—London, Brighton, and South Coast.

Miles from London Bdg.	Down.	Week Days.																					
	West End Station.	mrn	mrn	mrn	a	mrn	mrn	mrn	mrn	mrn	mrn	mrn	mrn	mrn	mrn	a	aft	non	aft	aft	aft	aft	aft
	VICTORIA ....dep.		5 25	6 45	7 23	7 40				9 10			9 45		1040	1110		12 0	12 5			1 25	
	Clapham Junction..dep.		5 32	6 52	7 30	7 47				9 17			9 52		1047	1117		12 7	1213			1 32	
	LONDON BRIDGE (C)dp	5 20		6 40	7 25		8 7		9 5				9 51		1045	1050		1150		1225	1250	1 27	1 40
2¾	New Cross	5 26			7 31								9 56			1057							
8½	Norwood Junction	5 43			7 44		8 25									1111		h					
10¼	East Croydon	5 50	6 0	7 11	7 58	8 11	8 31		9 25	9 38			1019		11 6	1134		1225	1230	1245	1 10	1 52	2 1
11¼	South Croydon		6 4	7 14		8 15	8 33			9 41			1023		11 9				1233	1248	1 12		2 4
11¾	Selsdon Road 277						8 36			9 43									1235				
12¾	Sanderstead						8 39			9 46					1113				1238		1 16		
15¼	Upper Warlingham *		6 14	7 25		8 24	8 48			9 54					1121				1246	1258	1 23		2 14
17	Woldingham		6 20				8 53			9 59		m					m		1251	1 4	1 28		
20¼	Oxted ¶		6 27	7 36		8 34	9 0	m		10 6	1012	1050			1131	1151	1225		1258	1 11	1 35		2 23
25½	Edenbridge Town		6 37			8 45		9 16		1017		11 4				12 2	1239			1 21			2 34
27¾	Hever		6 42			8 49		9 20		1021		11 8				b	1243			1 25			c
29¾	Cowden		6 48			8 54		9 25		1027		1113					1248			1 30			2 42
32	Ashurst ....[196		6 53			9 0		9 31		1033		1119					1254			1 36			
34½	Groombridge ◆ 191,		6 59			9 6		9 36		1040		1124				1217	1259			1 42			2 52
37½	Tunbridge Wells 240 a		7 10			9 14		9 44		1049		1131				1225	1 6			1 50			3 0
26¼	Lingfield			7 48			9 11				1022				1143				1 10		1 46		Except Saturdays.
27¾	Dormans			7 53			9 16				1027				1148				1 15		1 51		
30	East Grinstead ....arr.			8 0			9 23				1033		m	m	1154				1 22		1 58		
29¼	Three Bridges ...dep.	7 10			9 2				1012				1112	1130				1 5			Saturdays only.	2 33	
31½	Rowfant	7 16			9 8				1018				1120	1137				1 11				2 39	
33¾	Grange Road	7 22			9 14				1024				1126	1143				1 17				2 45	
36	East Grinstead ..arr.	7 30			9 22				1032				1133	1150				1 25				2 52	
—	East Grinstead ....dep.	7 40		8 16			9 35		1035					12 5					1 28			2 54	
35¼	Forest Row †	7 47		8 24			9 42		1043					1213					1 35			3 2	
36¾	Hartfield			8 32			9 50		1051					1221					1 43			3 10	
38	Withyham			8 36			9 54		1055					1225					1 46			3 14	
40½	Groombridge ◆ 191,196			8 42			10 0		11 1					1231					1 52			3 20	
43½	Tunbridge Wells 240 ar			8 50			1010		11 9					1238					2 0			3 28	

West End Station.	aft	aft	aft	a	aft	aft	aft	aft	aft	aft	aft	aft	aft	aft	aft	aft	aft	aft	aft	aft	aft	aft	aft
VICTORIA ....dep.		2 3		2 35	2 25		3 45	4 0				4 50			5 3			5 50		6 3	6 3		6 45
Clapham Junction..dep.		2 12			2 32			4 8							5 10					6 10	6 10		6 52
LONDON BRIDGE (C)dp	1 40		2k 3	2 25		2 57		4 5	4 10	4 22	4 47			5 l 5	5 10	5 22				6 8	6 8	6 39	7 0
New Cross			2k 9	2 31																			
Norwood Junction			2k27	2 43		3 13																	
East Croydon	2 1	2 28	2k31	2 55	2 57	3 19		4 29	4 31	4 42	5 4				5 31	5 42		6 r9		6 28	6 30	6 57	7 19
South Croydon	2 4		2k40	2 57	3 1	3 21			4 34	4 44					5 34	5 45				6 31	6 33	6 59	7 22
Selsdon Road 277		Stop			3 3	3 24			4 37						5 37					6 34		7 2	
Sanderstead	2 8			3 2	3 6	3 27			4 40	4 48					5 40	5 49				6 37		7 5	7 25
Upper Warlingham *	2 16	aft		3 9	3 14	3 35			4 48	4 55	5 14	5 20			5 48	5 57		6 22		6 44		7 13	7 32
Woldingham	2 21	m			3 19	3 40			4 53	5 0			m		5 53	6 1			m	6 49			7 37
Oxted ◆	2 28	2 30		3 18	3 26	3 47			5 0	5 7	5 23	5 29	5 33		6 0	6 8	6 11	6 32	6 38	6 56		7 22	7 44
Edenbridge Town	2 37			3 29	3 37	Saturdays only.				5 19	5 33	5 40				6 17			6 52	7 5			
Hever	c				3 42					5 23		5 44				6 21			6 56	7 9			
Cowden	2 45			3 37	3 47					5 28		5 48				6 26			7 1	7 14			
Ashurst ....[196					3 53							5 54				6 32			7 7	7 20			
Groombridge ◆ 191,	2 55			3 47	3 59		4 41			5 37	5 47	6 0				6 38			7 12	7 26			
Tunbridge Wells 240 ar	3 3			3 55	4 7		4 50			5 45	5 55	6 8				6 46				7 35			
Lingfield	Saturdays only.	2 44			3 46				5 10				5 45				6 21	6 42				7 34	
Dormans		2 49			3 51				5 15				5 50				6 26	6 47				7 39	
East Grinstead ....arr.		2 56	m		3 58				5 22				5 57				6 33	6 55				7 46	
Three Bridges ...dep.		Runs 5 minutes later on Sats.	3 35	Saturdays only.				5 7			Except Saturdays.			5 53							7 35	Except Saturdays.	
Rowfant			3 42					5 13						5 59							7 41		
Grange Road			3 48					5 19						6 5							7 47		
East Grinstead ..arr.			3 55					5 26						6 12							7 55		
East Grinstead ....dep.			4 6						5 30						6 13			6 56			7 56		
Forest Row †			4 13						5 37						6 21			7 2			8 3		
Hartfield									5 45									7 10			8 11		
Withyham									5 49									7 13			8 14		
Groombridge ◆ 191,196									5 55									7 19			8 20		
Tunbridge Wells 240 ar									6 3									7 27			8 28		

m Motor Cars—One class only

Oxted towards East Grinstead

OXTED

1. The trackwork and main buildings remain unaltered today, 60 years after this photograph was taken. This northward view is from the signal box steps, the handrails of which are seen in the foreground. The bay platform was for many years used for the direct stopping train service to Tunbridge Wells. Note the early Stroudley 4-wheeled 3rd class brake in the siding. (Late E. Wallis)

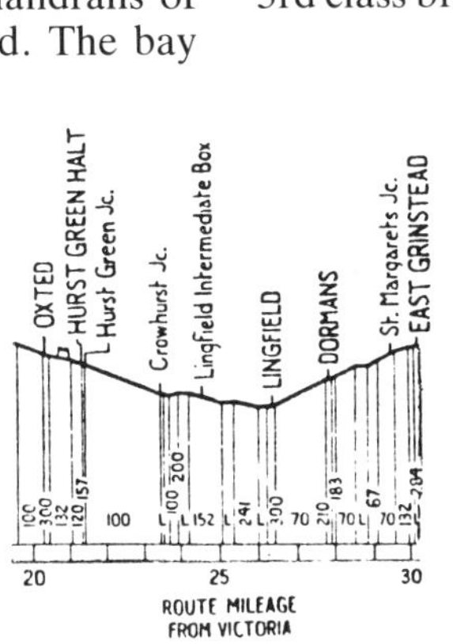

Bradshaw 1910

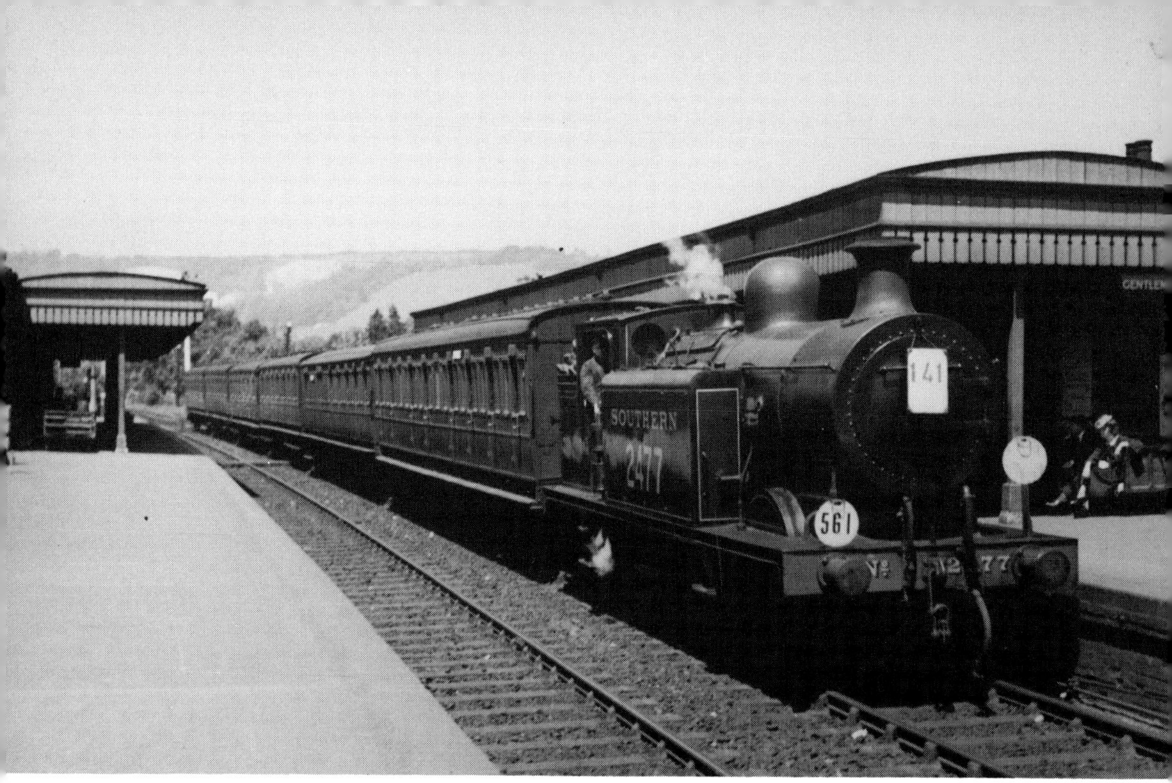

2. On a brilliant summer's day in 1939, a smart 0–6–2 tank of class E4X arrives with a train of assorted compartment coaches from London Bridge, on a bank holiday special. The quarry of Oxted Lime Works is visible in the distant North Downs and even then passengers had to sit on luggage trucks due to insufficient platform seats. (F.M. Gates/Lens of Sutton)

J. KIMMINGS,

OXTED RAILWAY STATION,

Job Master & Cab Proprietor

A Conveyance runs Twice Daily from this Station to Westerham

All Trains met up or down. Open and Close Conveyances.

Orders received by the Station Master.

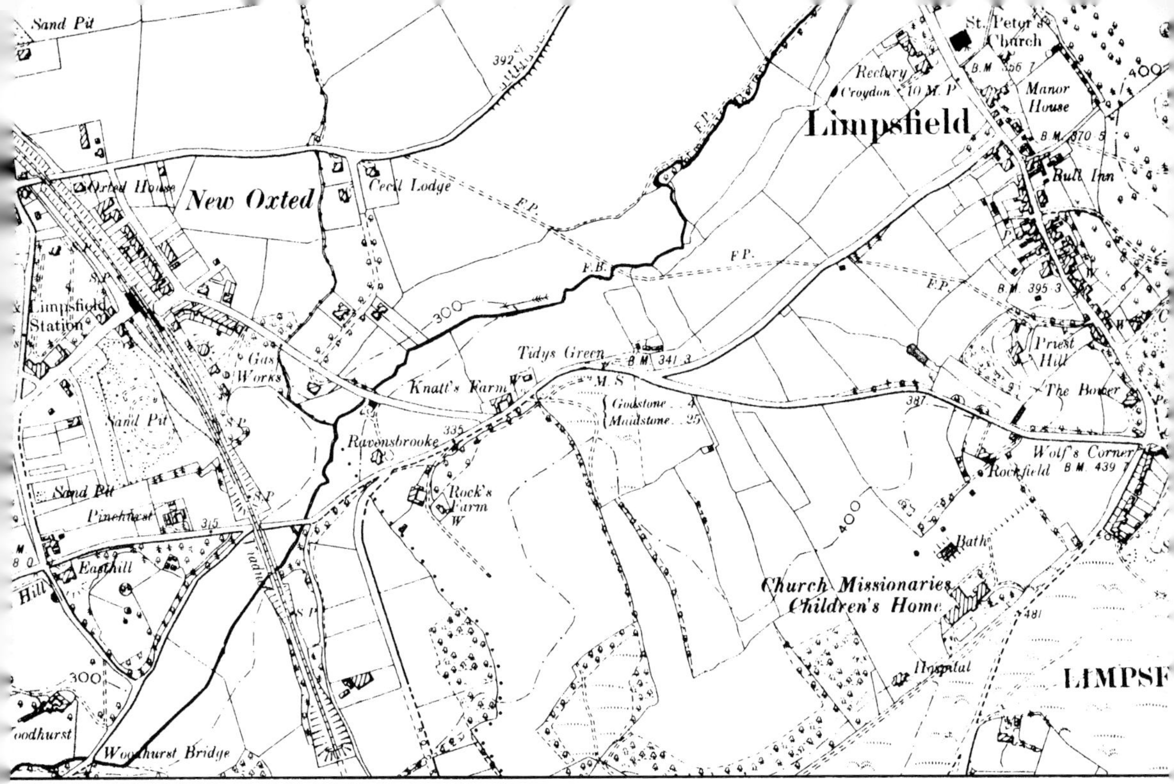

1898 map, six inches to the mile scale.

3. Class 4 no. 42067 takes refreshment after arriving with the 2.8 p.m. train from Victoria on 1st August 1955. The Maunsell coaches are painted in "plum and custard" livery. The push-pull in the bay is close to the main water tank, which supplied the water crane by underground pipe. (J.H. Aston)

4. Former LBSCR class C2X (BR no. 32548) leaves the head shunt of this rather cramped goods yard on 19th July 1961. The signal box is unchanged today, although it now controls mainly colour light signals, only the two down starters now being semaphore. (R.S. Greenwood)

(M. Papps)

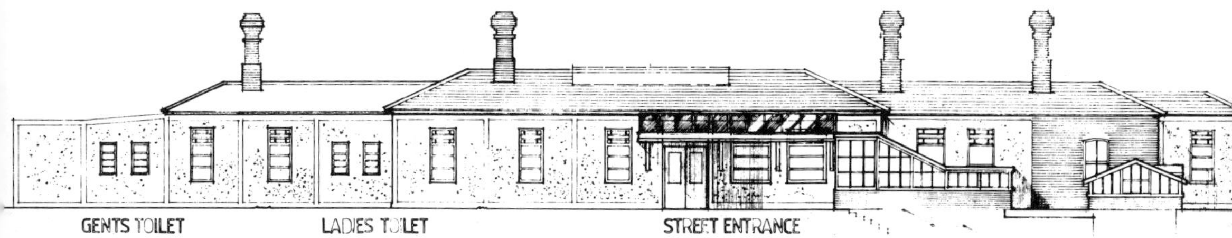

5. The H class 0–4–4 tanks of the SECR were ideal for push-pull working. The end handrail of the coach is on the extreme right of the picture. Nearest to the camera is the Westinghouse steam operated air compressor and on the end of the side tank is the steam operated reverser, a feature of SECR locomotives. (E. Wilmshurst)

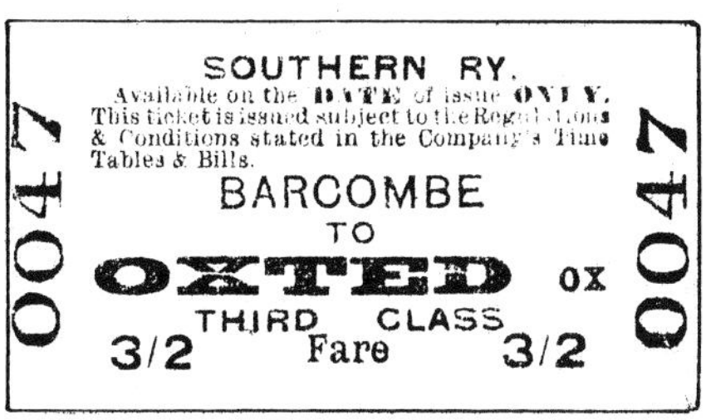

(M. Papps)

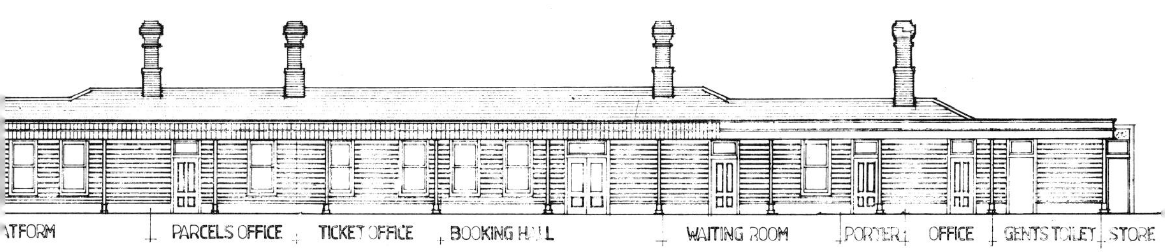

HURST GREEN

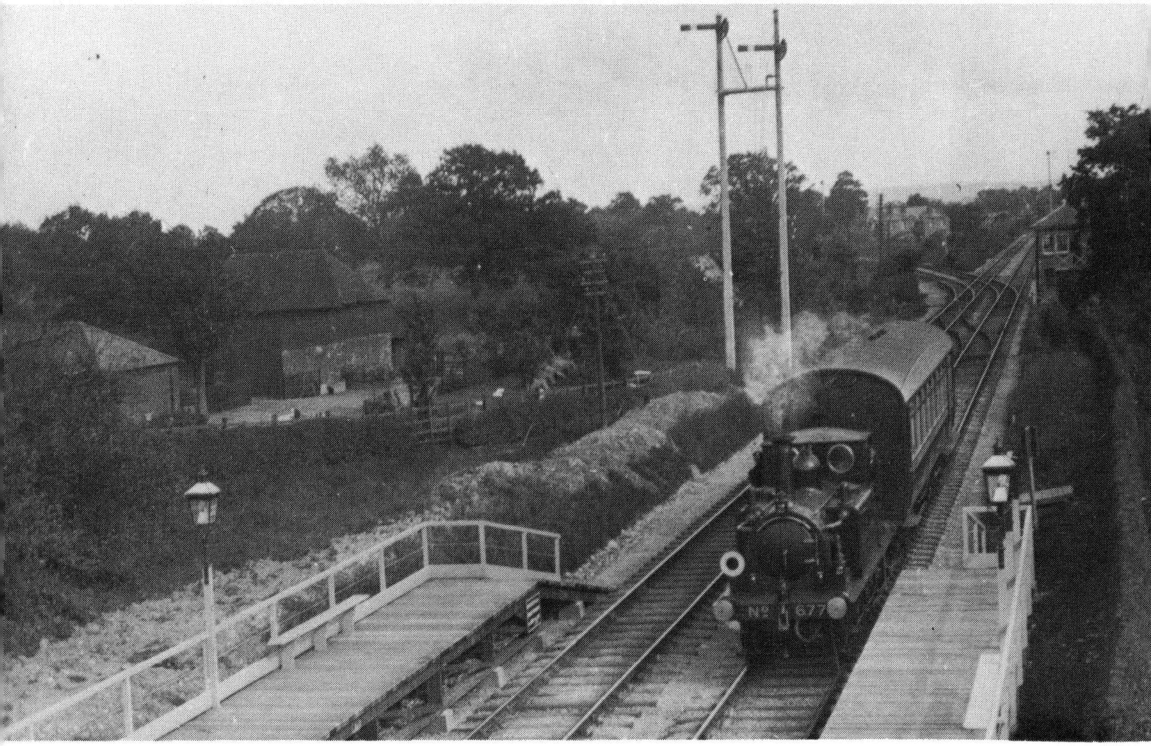

6. Rebuilt Terrier no.677, formerly *Wonersh*, with the Oxted motor train entering Hurst Green Halt. Hurst Green Junction is in the background, the line on the left is to Edenbridge and today carries the Uckfield trains, whilst the line straight on is to East Grinstead. The halt was opened on 1st June 1907 and was initially served by trains of the type shown here. (Lens of Sutton)

Map of 1898 – scale six inches to one mile.

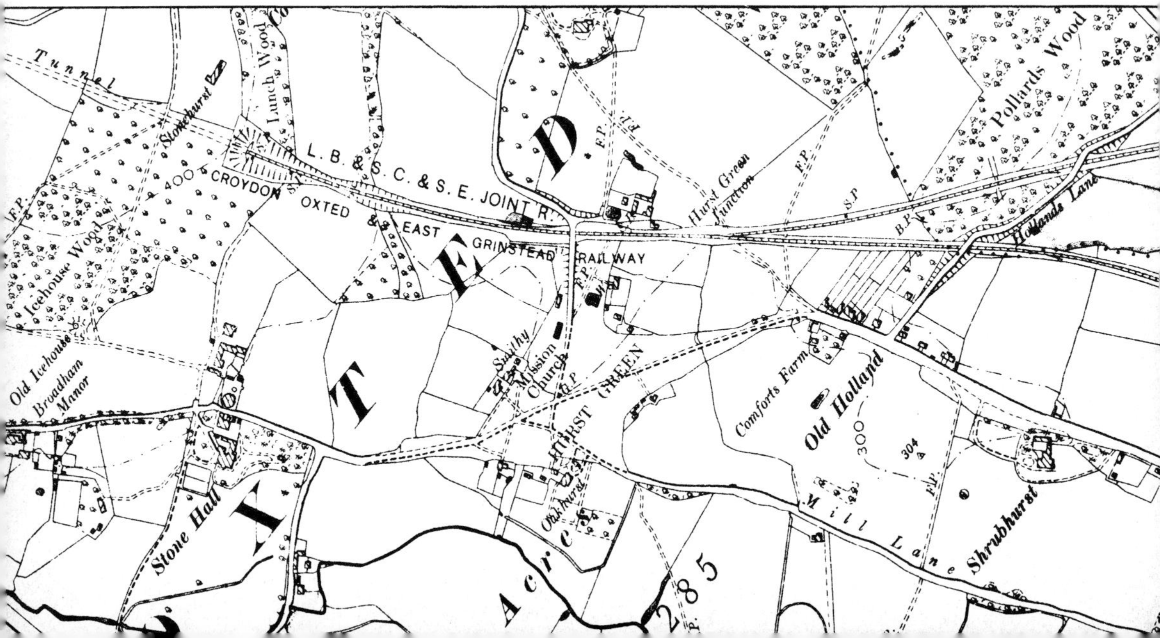

7. Oxted to Tunbridge Wells train leaving on 14th April 1961, headed by H class tank no. 31522. In the foreground is the original Halt platform whilst under the bridge the new station can be seen under construction. (P. Hay)

8. Framed by the road bridge, we see the present concrete and brick station, which accommodates 12 coaches. Extensive post war residential development in the area has made this a busy station. It was opened on 12th June 1961 and the title 'Halt' was dropped. (J. Scrace)

9. The signal box was photographed on 16th June 1923 when relief signalman E. Brown was on duty. It has changed little in the ensuing years, except that the ventilator has assumed a curious angle which can be seen in the next picture. (Late E. Wallis)

10. This engineers train had to adopt a circuitous route for its journey from Newhaven to Crowborough, via Croydon on 7th April 1979. The diesel locomotive is no. 33065 and it is now heading south towards Edenbridge. (J. Scrace)

11. The lines on the right were constructed as a spur connecting the SER's Redhill to Tonbridge with SER/LBSCR joint line from Oxted. The train is running from Victoria to Tunbridge Wells West via East Grinstead on 24th March 1962, headed by BR standard class 4 tank no. 80059. Most services over the spur ceased on 10th June 1955, but it continued to be used by diverted trains for some time. (E. Wilmshurst)

Timetable for 1924

LONDON, THREE BRIDGES, EAST GRINSTEAD, and TUNBRIDGE WELLS WEST.—Southern.

Week Days.

Miles from Lond'n Bg.	Down.	mrn	mrn	mrn	mrn	mrn	mrn	mrn	mrn	mrn		mrn	mrn	mrn	mrn		mrn	mrn	mrn	mrn	aft	mrn	mrn	aft	mrn	aft		aft	aft	aft	aft
	VICTORIA (W. End) dep.		5 30		6 37			7 10					8 55							11 15			1155		1155						
	Clapham Junction .. "		5 37		6 44			7 15					9 1							11 22			12 2		12 2						
	East Croydon ...... arr.		5 55		7 0			7 33					9 16							11 37			1219		1219						
	LONDON BD. (C.) dep.	5 18						7 20	8 7			8 40			9 18		1010		1050			1110		1210	1220	1250		1A30	1 38		1 38
2	New Cross Gate .. "	5 28						7 26							9 25																
8	Norwood Junction § ..	5 42						7 39	8 25						9 49																
10	East Croydon .... arr.	5 48						7 44	8 30			8 58			9 54		1027		11 7			1127		1227	1240	1 8		1 49	1 56		1 59
—	East Croydon ...... dep.	5 50	5 58		7 3			7 50	8 32			9 1	9 18		9 55		1028		11 8	11 38		1128	1223	1228	1241	1 9		1 50	1 58		2 1
11	South Croydon		6 1		7 6				8 35				9 21		9 57				1111				1226		1244	1 11			2 1		2 5
11	Selsdon Road								8 37														1228					1 53			
12	Sanderstead								8 40				9 25		10 1				1115				1231		1249	1 15		1 56	2 5		2 9
15	Upper Warlingham * ..		6 10		7 15				8 48				9 33						1123				1239		1257	1 22		2 3	2 12		2 16
17	Woldingham		6 16		7 20				8 53				9 38						1128				1244		1 3	1 27		2 8	2 17		2 21
20	Oxted ** .... arr.		6 23		7 27				9 0				9 45						1135	11 55			1251		1 11	1 34		2 15	2 24		2 23
—	Oxted .... dep.		6 25			7 40				9 5			9 46					1042		11 56	1225				1 12				2 26		2 30
21	Hurst Green Halt					7 43				9 8								1046			1228										
23	Monks Lane Halt					7 48												1051			1233										
25	Edenbridge Town †† ..		6 36			7 54				9 16			9 57					1056		12 6	1238				1 21	Saturdays only.		Saturdays only.	2 37	Except Saturdays.	2 41
27	Hever		6 41			7 58				9 20			10 1					11 0		12B10	1242				1 25				2 42		2 46
29	Cowden		6 46			8 3				9 25			10 7					11 5			1247				1 30				2 47		2 51
32	Ashurst		6 52			8 9				9 31			1013					1111			1253				1 36				2 53		2 57
—	Ashurst ...... dep.		6 53			8 9				9 31			1017					1111			1253				1 37				2 54		2 58
34	Groombridge 224 ..		7 0			8 14				9 36			1024					1116			1258				1 44				3 0		3 4
35	High Rocks Halt					8 18				9 40								1120													
37	Tunbdg Wlls W. arr.		7 7			8 22				9 45			1032					1124			1 6				1 51				3 7		3 11
—	Eridge 223 to 225 arr.		7 6										1021							12 22											
—	Oxted ¶ .... dep.				7 28				9 1					10 3					1136				1252			1 35		2 20		2 30	
21	Hurst Green Halt													10 5														2 22		2 33	
26	Lingfield				7 39				9 12					1014					1145				1 3		Saturdays only.	1 45		2 31	Except Saturdays.	2 42	Saturdays only.
27	Dormans				7 44				9 17					1019					1151				1 8			1 50		2 36		2 47	
30	East Grinstead .... arr.				7 50				9 24					1025					1158				1 15			1 57		2 45		2 54	
29	Three Bridges	7 5		7 30			8 25	9 0				10 5					1125					1 3		1 30							
31	Rowfant	7 12		7 37			8 32	9 11				1011					1131					1 9		1 37							
33	Grange Road ‖ ... [222	7 17		7 42			8 37	9 16				1016					1135					1 15		1 42							
36	East Grinstead arr.	7 23		7 48			8 43	9 23				1023					1141					1 22		1 48							
—	East Grinstead .... dep.	7 25			8 15				9 31			1029		1029									1 25			1 58					
35	Forest Row †	7 33			8 23				9 39			1037		1037									1 34			2 5					
36	Hartfield				8 31				9 47			1045		1045									1 4[illegible]			2 13					
38	Withyham				8 35				9 51			1049		1049									1 46			2 17					
40	Groombridge 220, 224				8 42				9 53			1056		1056									1 53			2 23					
43	Tunbdg Wlls W. 270 arr.				8 49				10 5			11 3		11 3									2 0			2 30					

Through Train to Uckfield and Heathfield Lines, see pages 223 and 224

Leaves Cannon Street at 12 16 aft. and calls at London Bridge (H. L.)

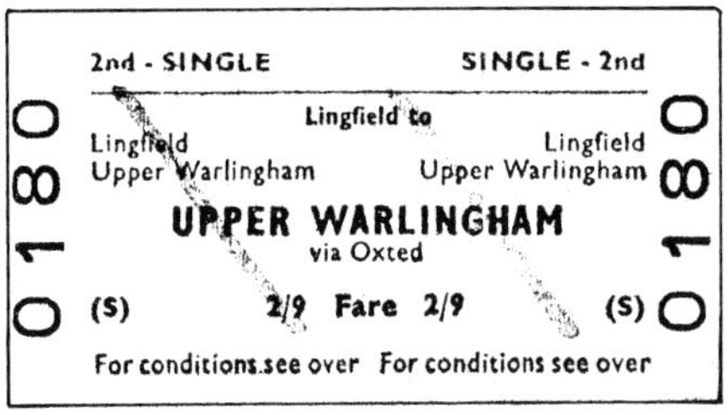

2nd - SINGLE SINGLE - 2nd

0180 Lingfield to 0180

Lingfield Lingfield

Upper Warlingham Upper Warlingham

UPPER WARLINGHAM

via Oxted

(S) 2/9 Fare 2/9 (S)

For conditions see over For conditions see over

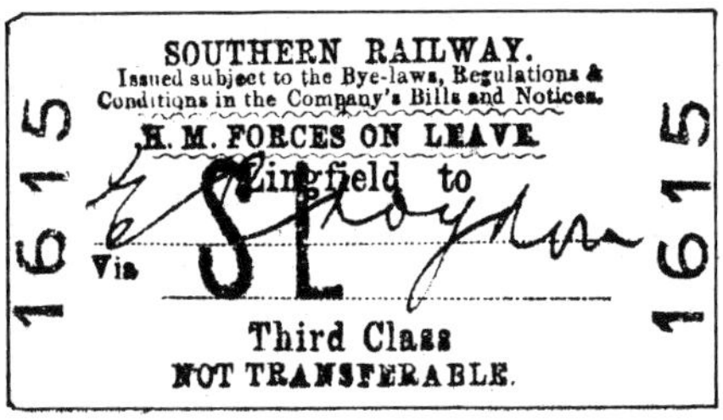

SOUTHERN RAILWAY.

Issued subject to the Bye-laws, Regulations & Conditions in the Company's Bills and Notices.

1615 H. M. FORCES ON LEAVE 1615

Lingfield to

Via

Third Class

NOT TRANSFERABLE.

Map 1912.

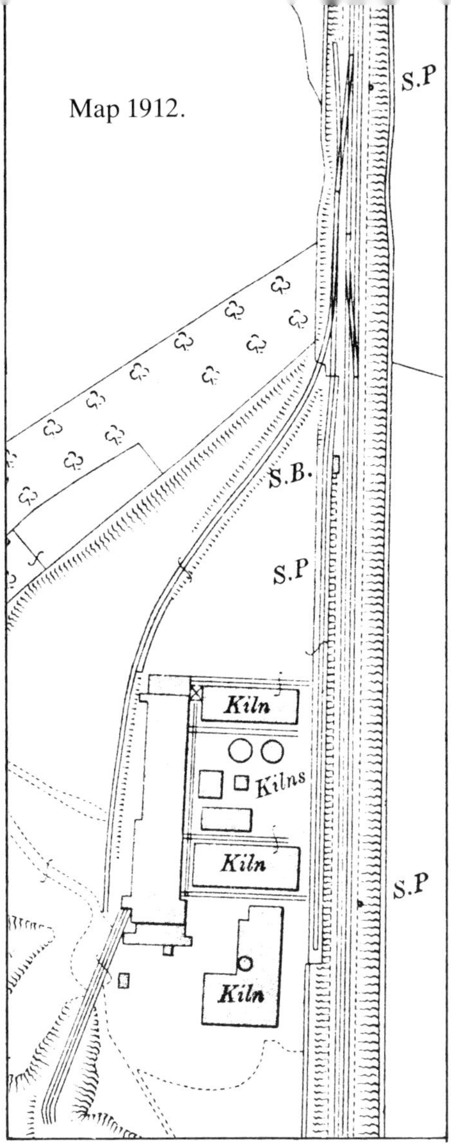

12. Lingfield Intermediate Box, looking north in 1951. The bridge still carries the lane to Chellows Farm but the box and the white gates no longer exist. The gates were across a private siding to Crowhurst Brick & Tile Works which ceased production in 1980, although rail traffic to it had stopped many years earlier. (Pamlin Prints)

LINGFIELD

13. A northward view of the station prior to its opening in May 1884. The covering of sleepers with ballast was later banned by the Railway Inspectorate of the Board of Trade, as it could conceal defective timber. The platform on the right became an island platform in 1894, a racecourse having been opened nearby in 1890. (Lens of Sutton)

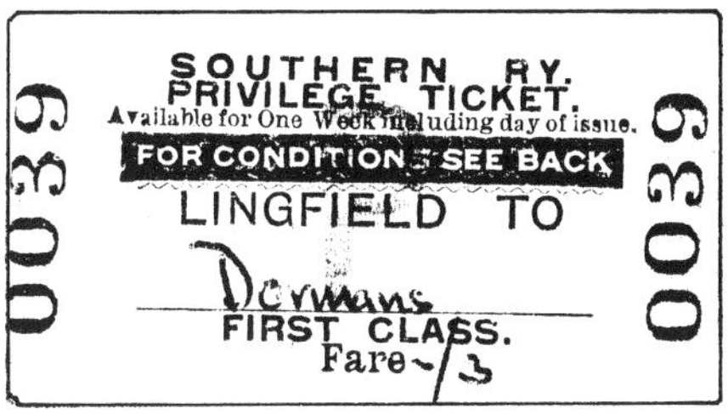

14. The prospective passenger's view as shown on a Frith's post card, franked 8 PM - 13 NOV - 1916. (E. Jackson Collection)

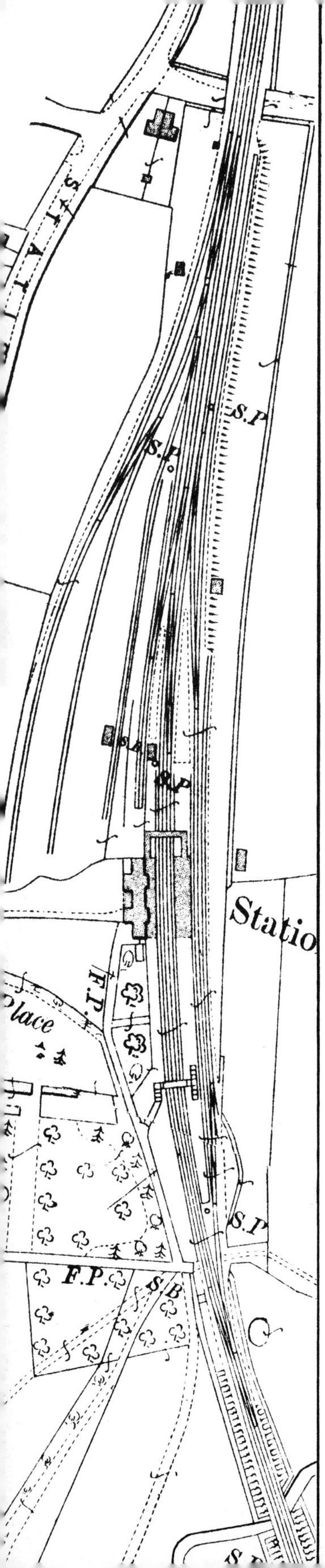

Map 1912.

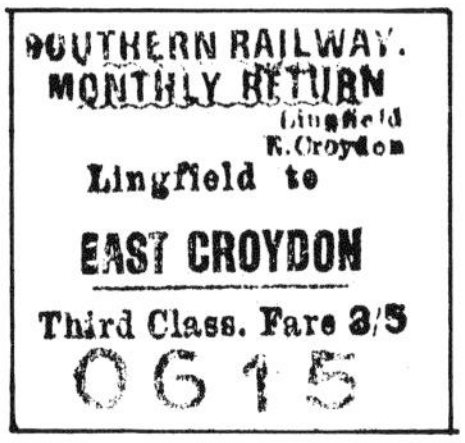

15. Ex-LBSCR Class 13 4–4–2 tank no. 2026 on a Lingfield Race Special, in 1938. The train, all first class, was made up of the former *City Limited* stock. Many extra trains were run on race days, including the Pullman in the background. During the races, the locomotives were coupled together and taken on to East Grinstead for water and turning. The latter involved running through the low-level platforms, reversing through the goods yards and returning via the high-level station and St. Margarets spur. (E.R. Lacey/R.C. Riley Collection)

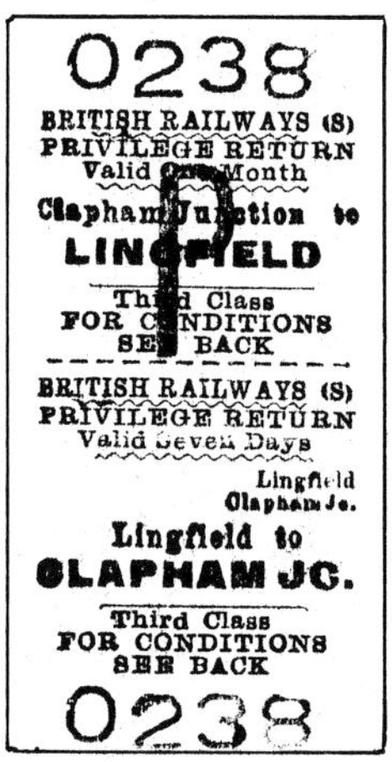

17. DEMU no. 1118 forming the 11.09 Victoria–East Grinstead train passes the 50 mph speed restriction sign on the 7th June 1969. The sheds in the background are for banana ripening and until 1st October 1971 van trains from Avonmouth Docks were run regularly for this special traffic. The general goods yard closed in 1968 and whilst the up platform buildings largely remain intact, the down platform now only bears a 'bus shelter'. The signal box is currently the only one still open (part time only) between Hurst Green and the end of the line. (J. Scrace)

16. Racegoers were provided with a covered way to the race course (on the left) and an additional down platform canopy, with a second footbridge. The latter has been removed to Sheffield Park for the eventual benefit of admirers of the iron horse. (J. Scrace)

DORMANS

18. The century old station building with its elegant round-headed windows and ornate chimneys still stands today. Their location at right angles to the track is unusual. The tapered white post is that of the down starting signal, standing in the cutting. At one period there was a siding for Dormans Park, ½ mile south of the station on the up side. (Lens of Sutton)

Map 1912.

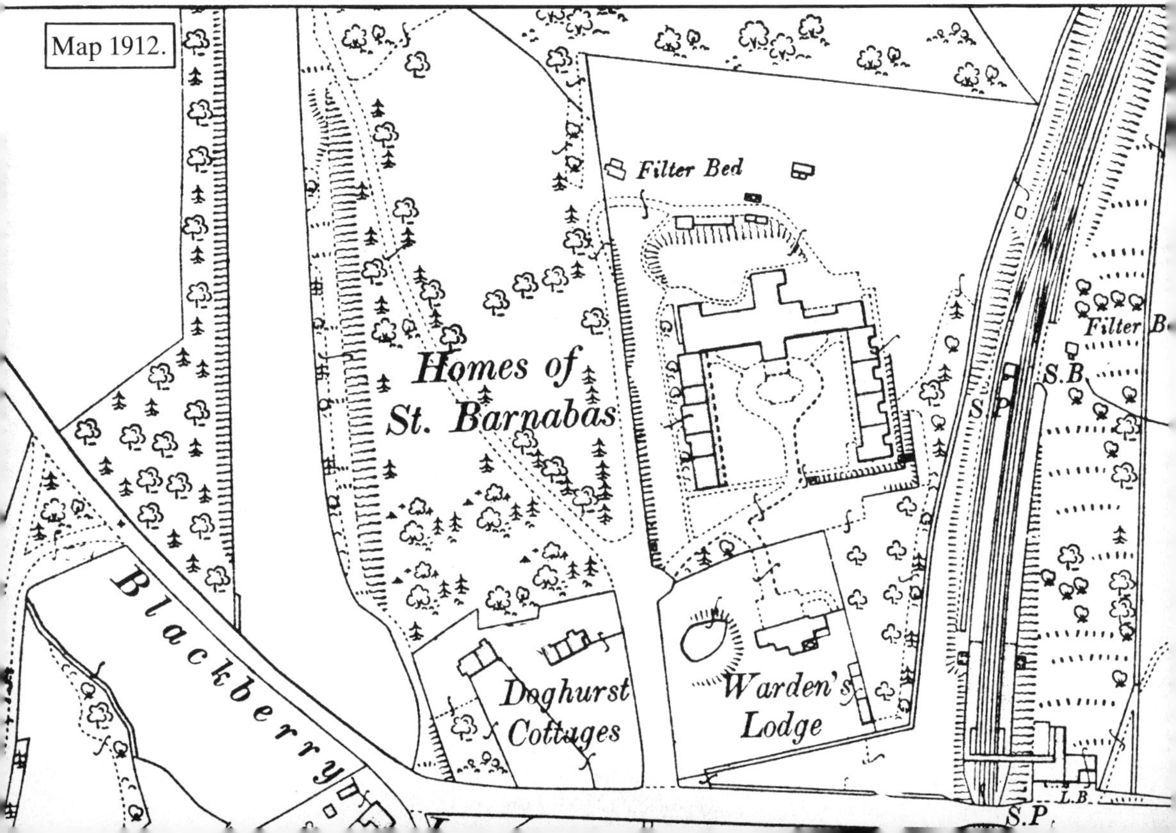

19. The comforts of weather protection and a gentleman's toilet have all gone – at least there are still trains – and these have both. On the down side the inclined footway retains a roof (a blessing in the snow) but the platform only possesses a bus shelter. (R.C. Riley Collection)

20. Class K 2–6–0 no. 32352 crosses Cooks Pond Viaduct on 12th June 1950 with a Haywards Heath–London Bridge train. Although it appears to be a massive river it is only a pond, fed by quite a small stream. The attractive lattice design was favoured by the engineer of the line, James Firbank, and was used for all major bridges from Croydon to East Grinstead. (S.C. Nash)

Three Bridges towards East Grinstead

THREE BRIDGES

22. On the other side of the shed seen in the previous photograph, poor old *Millwall* was in steam every day but never went anywhere. It remained static from July 1901 until October 1905 supplying steam for a water pump. Notice that its own water supply was permanently piped in to its side tank.
(E.R. Lacey Collection)

. Looking north from the signal box wards London, in about 1908, it is apparent at the station had four platforms before the ain line was quadrupled. The one on the ft was for the Horsham branch whilst the y on the right was for the East Grinstead ains. On the extreme left is the locomotive ed which was demolished when the lines ere widened. A turntable and a single road ed were provided in between the Horsham d Brighton lines, where a new 3-road shed as erected in about 1909.
ate E. Wallis Collection)

3. L.A. Brighty, the upright station master Three Bridges in the early years of the outhern Railway. (B.C. Vigor Collection)

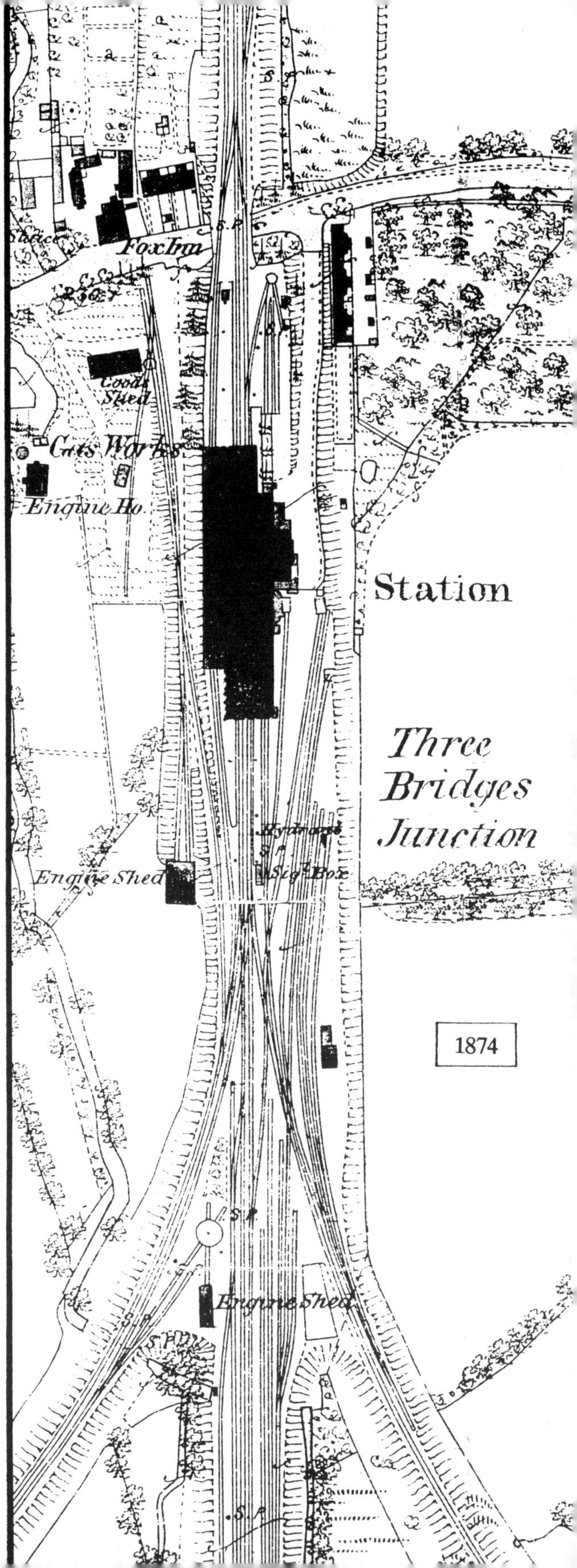

24. The new platforms and canopies can be seen in the distance in this April 1934 view. The old signals remained although electric trains had commenced running from London on 17th July 1932 and were extended to Brighton and West Worthing on 1st January 1933. A motor train for East Grinstead stands in the partly rebuilt bay platform. (Late E. Wallis Collection)

25. Looking northwards towards the station, on the left margin of the picture is part of the locomotive hoist; next the curved roof of the machine shop; behind it is the water tower; in the centre is the main 3-road through shed and on the right is the coaling stage and crane. A 60 ft turntable was provided. The depot closed in June 1964. (Lens of Sutton)

26. H class no. 31551 glides almost silently (due to the muffling effect of over a foot of snow) into the bay with the 2.27 pm departure from East Grinstead, on 29th December 1962. The following 10 weeks were to be the severest the south had experienced in living memory, with almost no thaw. The new signalling centre has recently been built at this location. (E. Wilmshurst)

27. Another H class tank, this time about to pull its train out from under that most civilised station feature – the cosy overall station roof, unchanged since the first photograph in this section was taken. The driver watches for the right-away, as he would not hear the guard whilst his charge blows off. (C.R.L. Coles)

28. The earliest known view of the crossing keeper's cottage, with many unanswered questions. Was the keeper a widow? Was she putting her hand on her only son's shoulder as he went to his first job? Was it his first new suit? Was the flag red to stop the train to take him to his new job?
(Late E. Wallis Collection)

Bradshaw 1869

LONDON, EAST GRINSTEAD, and TUNBRIDGE WELLS.—London, Brighton, and South Coast.

Miles from London Bridge.*	Fares from London Bridge. 1 cl. s. d.	2 cl. s. d.	3 cl. s. d.	Down.	Week Days. 1,2,3 mrn	1&2 mrn	1&2 aft	1&2 aft	1,2,3 aft	Sndys 1,2,3 mrn	1,2,3 aft
				Kensington .. (Deps.—Local Trains, p. 48.)	7 30	1126	3 53	....	6 15	....	5 22
				West Brompton	7 33	1129	3 56	....	6 18	....	5 25
				Chelsea	7 35	1131	3 58	....	6 29	....	5 28
				Victoria	7 40	1150	4 0	4 55	6 35	6 55	6 30
				Clapham Junc.	7 48	1159	4 9	....	6 43	7 3	5 40
	....	....	....	London Bridge.,	8 0	12 0	4 10	5 0	6 45	7 15	6 35
	....	....	....	Norwood Junc ..	7 59	12 0	....	....	....	7 18	....
	....	....	....	Croydon (East)..	8 28	1226	4 31	5 21	7 10	7 38	6 59
	....	....	....	Caterham Junc..	....	....	....	....	....	....	....
	....	....	....	Red Hill Junc...	8 50	1247	....	....	....	8 1	7 20
	....	....	....	Earlswood	8 53	....	....	....	....	....	....
	....	....	....	Horley	9 2	....	....	....	....	8 15	....
31¾	....	....	....	Three Bridges ..	9 20	1 8	5 2	5 50	7 50	9 30	7 45
33¾	6 3	4 10	2 7	Rowfant	9 25	1 13	5 7	5 55	7 55	9 35	7 50
36	6 8	5 2	2 9	Grange Road	9 30	1 18	5 12	6 0	8 0	9 40	7 55
	7 3	5 8	3 0	East Grinstead	9 41	1 29	5 22	6 10	8 11	9 53	8 5
39¼	7 10	6 1	3 8	Forest Row	9 49	1 37	5 30	....	8 19	9 58	8 13
42¼	8 5	6 7	3 6	Hartfield	9 57	1 45	5 38	....	8 27	10 6	8 21
44	8 8	6 9	3 8	Withyham	10 0	1 48	5 41	....	8 30	10 9	8 24
46½	9 3	6 9	3 9	Groombge [73, 64, 66	10 5	1 53	5 46	....	8 35	1014	8 29
49½	9 6	6 9	3 9	Tunbridge Wells arr	1013	2 1	5 54	....	8 43	1022	8 37

Up.	Week Days. 1,2,3 mrn	1&2 mrn	1,2,3 mrn	1&2 aft	1,2,3 aft	Sndys 1,2,3 mrn	1,2,3 aft
Tunbridge Wells dep	7 45	....	1110	3 10	5 5[illegible]	7 10	5 46
Groombridge	7 52	....	1117	3 17	[illegible]	7 17	5 5[illegible]
Withyham	7 57	....	1123	3 22	6 10	7 22	5 58
Hartfield	8 1	....	1126	3 26	6 14	7 26	6 2
Forest Row	8 9	....	1134	3 [illegible]	[illegible]	7 42	6 1[illegible]
East Grinstead	8 19	10 0	1145	3 45	6 33	7 45	6 20
Grange Road	8 26	10 7	1152	3 52	6 40	7 52	6 27
Rowfant	8 31	1012	1157	3 57	6 45	7 57	6 32
Three Bridges 48 (Arrs.—Local Trains, p. 53.)	8 39	1020	12 5	4 5	6 53	8 5	6 40
Horley	8 55	....	....	....	7 12	....	....
Earlswood	....	....	....	4 32	7 22	....	....
Red Hill Jn. 64..	9 10	....	1237	4 38	7 28	9 40	7 5
Caterham Jn. 64	....	....	....	....	7 44	....	....
Croydon (East)..	9 29	1053	1 0	4 57	7 52	10 4	7 26
Norwood Jn. 59..	....	1124	....	5 4	7 58	....	....
London Bridge..	9 50	1110	1 20	5 27	8 22	1025	7 45
Clapham Jn. 36	....	1111	1 20	5 22	8 18	....	....
Victoria 110..	10 5	1118	1 27	5 30	8 25	1045	7 5[illegible]
Chelsea	1047	1119	2 19	5 41	8 49	1121	8 2[illegible]
West Brompton	1050	1122	2 22	5 49	8 52	1124	8 27
Kensingtn 125	1053	1125	2 25	5 53	8 55	1127	8 30

* The distances from Victoria are 35 chains further, and from Kensington 74 chains further.

ROWFANT

29. Land was often given to a new railway company in return for the provision of a station on an estate. In 1855, Curtis Miranda Lampson, an American fur trader, gave the land, and the railway provided this splendid little well-ornamented station, complete with a shelter for Lampson's coachmen (behind the nameboard), which was part of the agreement. The loop, footbridge and up platform with shelter were added in 1900-01. (M.G. Joly Collection)

30. Before the days of mass motoring, ramblers' excursions were widespread. This is a Victoria to Forest Row special, passing the former brickworks siding, on 16th September 1951. The locomotives are class N no. 31829 and class UI no. 31906. (S.C. Nash)

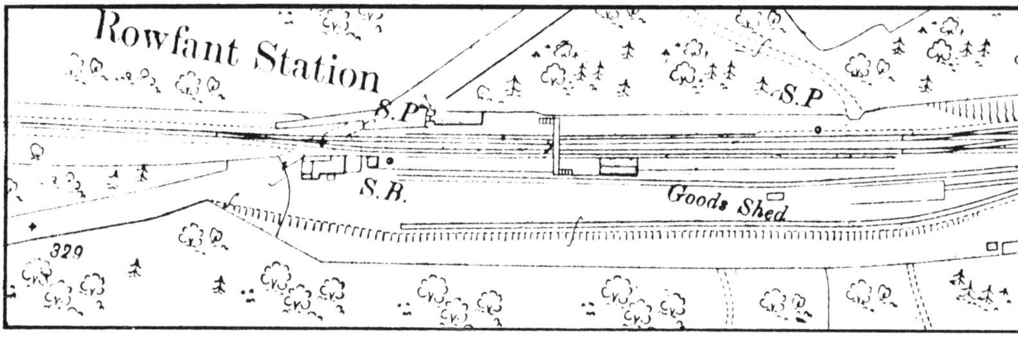
Rowfant Station
S.P
S.P
S.B.
Goods Shed
329

ROWFANT
WAY OUT
ROWFANT

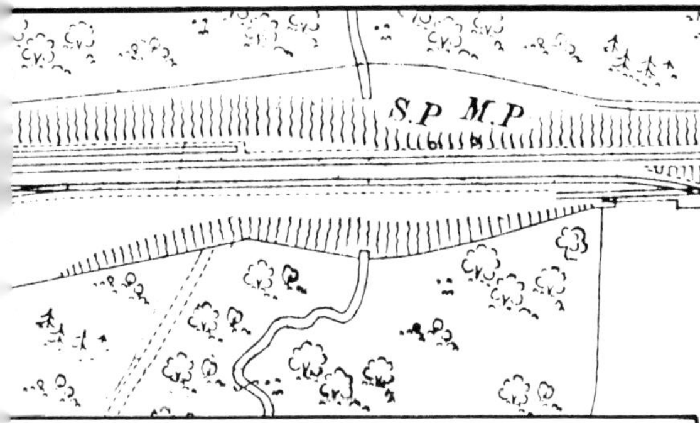
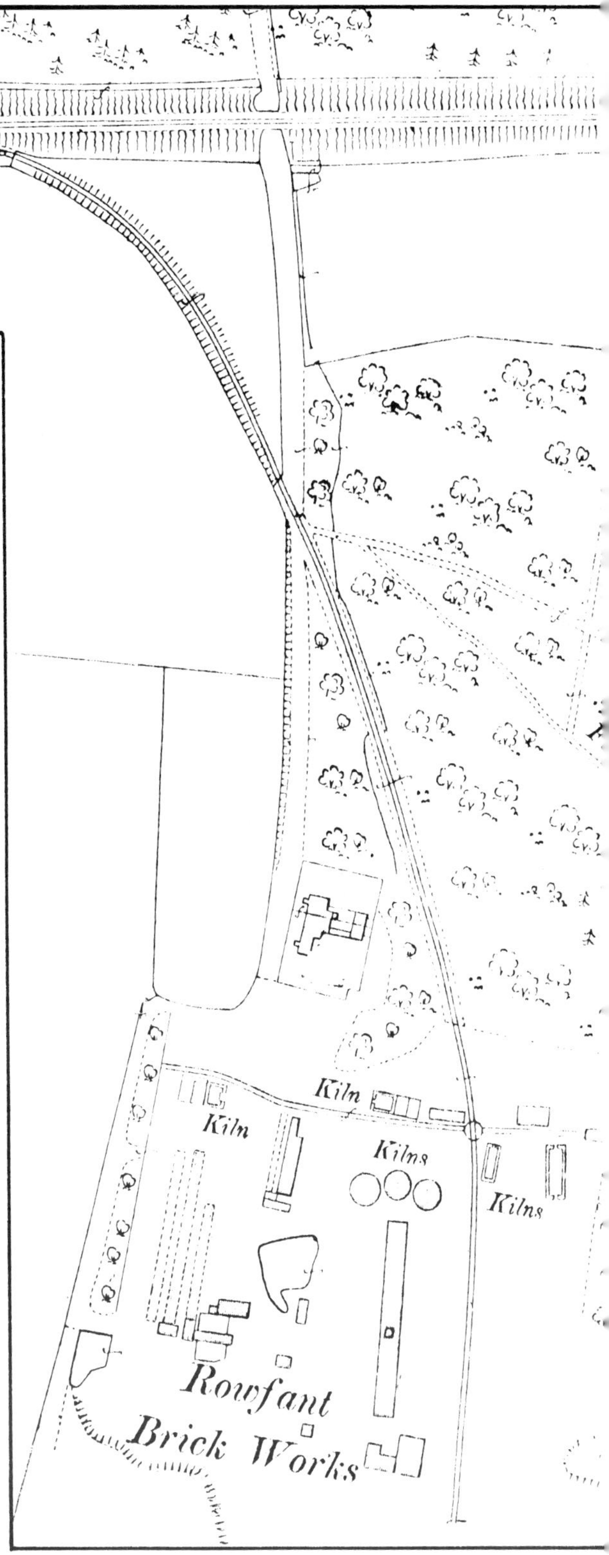

1910 map.

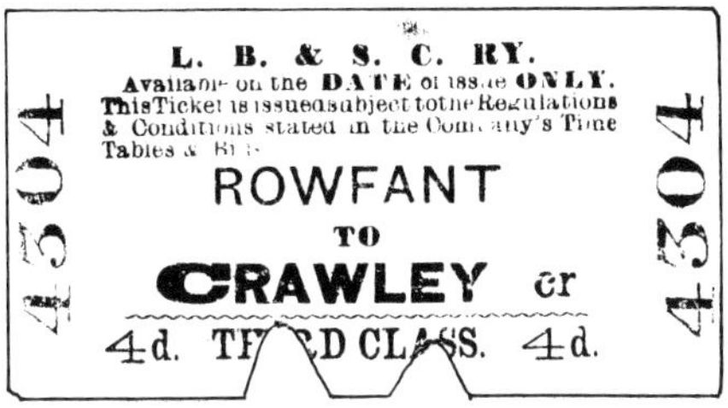

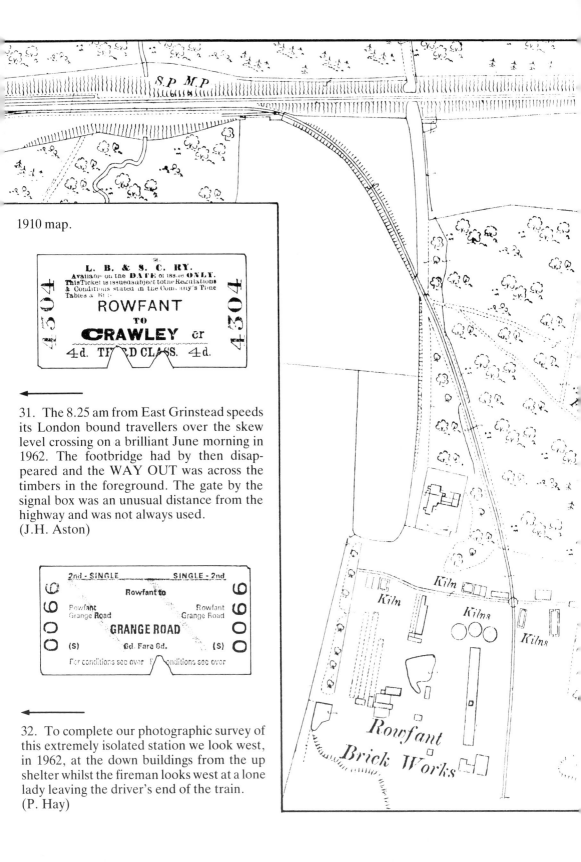

31. The 8.25 am from East Grinstead speeds its London bound travellers over the skew level crossing on a brilliant June morning in 1962. The footbridge had by then disappeared and the WAY OUT was across the timbers in the foreground. The gate by the signal box was an unusual distance from the highway and was not always used. (J.H. Aston)

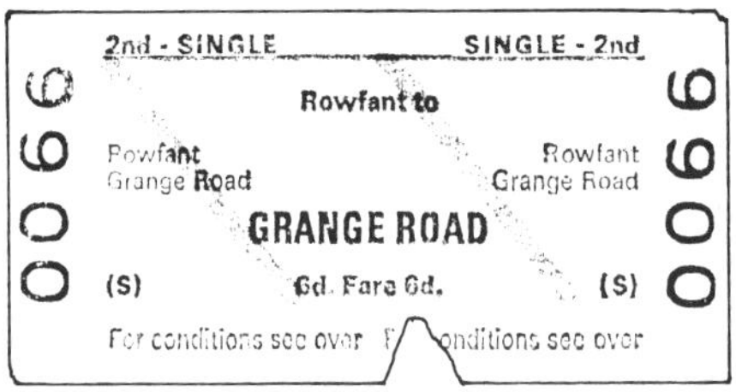

32. To complete our photographic survey of this extremely isolated station we look west, in 1962, at the down buildings from the up shelter whilst the fireman looks west at a lone lady leaving the driver's end of the train. (P. Hay)

GRANGE ROAD

Railway Station, Grange Rd.
Pub. by H. Lowman, Turners Hill

33. For many years this station had the lengthy title of "Grange Road for Crawley Down and Turners Hill". It was opened in March 1860 and enlarged in 1877-78. The footbridge seen in this local postcard was erected in 1897. (Lens of Sutton)

34. Class M7 no. 30055, passing steam from improper places, runs past the overgrown goods yard with the 1.08 pm Three Bridges to Tunbridge Wells West train on 19th May 1963. It was withdrawn from service four months later. (S.C. Nash)

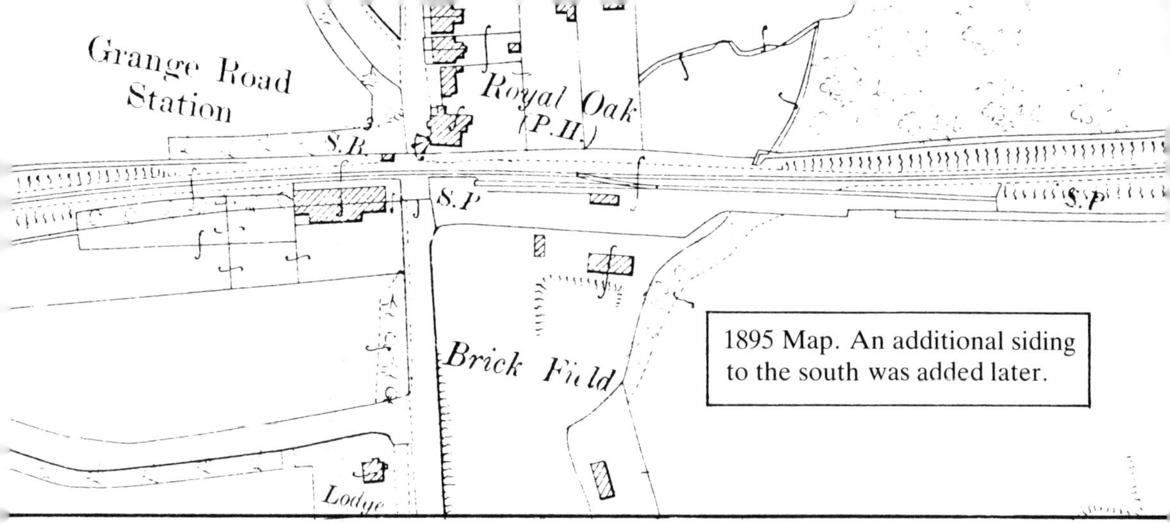

1895 Map. An additional siding to the south was added later.

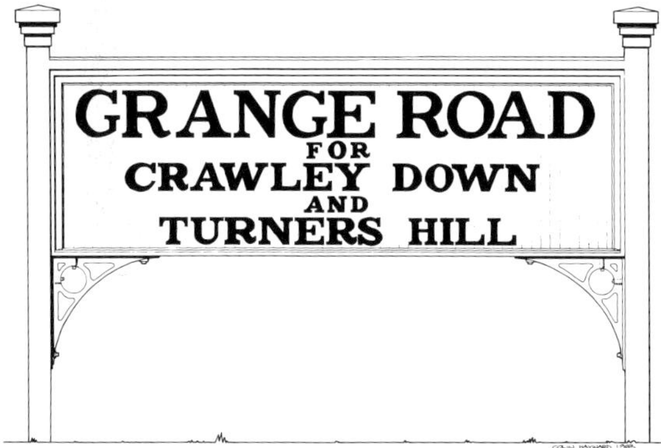

35. Diesel-electric units had been introduced by the time this picture of the 1.08 pm was taken in the following year, on 28th November (J. Scrace)

Lewes towards East Grinstead

LEWES

36. The first station in Lewes was opened in 1846 and was on the Brighton to St. Leonards line. We are looking westwards at the second station which was of Swiss chalet style and lasted from 1859 to 1889. This photograph was taken about 1888 and shows a train, on the left, from Brighton to Hastings headed by D class no. 297 *Bonchurch* with a Terrier class locomotive in the bay platform, behind which is a lantern roofed brake van of Craven design. On the right is the Victoria to Hastings train hauled by an 0–4–2. Maps and further photographs of this interesting junction appear in the *Brighton to Eastbourne* album of the *South Coast Railways Series.* (E.J. Bedford/Lens of Sutton)

37. The exterior of the third and present station as seen in the early part of this century. On the left of Station Road was a good source of railway revenue – the cattle market. (Lens of Sutton)

38. Lewes once required four signal boxes but this one alone is now sufficient. Viewed from the end of the present platform 6/7 in July 1923, we see on the left two horse boxes, once a common feature of the railway scene, and above them the bag of the locomotive water column. The lines diverge to the left to East Grinstead and Tunbridge Wells and to the right to Hastings and Seaford. Notice the name apparently cut into the chalk hill side. (Late E. Wallis)

39. With conductor rails already in place, we see one of the popular D3 tanks leaving with a Tunbridge Wells train in April 1935, three months before electric services commenced to the East Sussex coast. The leading coach is of the "Birdcage" type which gave the guard a look out along the roof. The west bound train consists of ex LBSC coaches. (S.W. Baker)

40. In November 1956, one coach of 1921 vintage was more than adequate for the small number of passengers offering themselves for transport south of East Grinstead. The goods engine provided was no. 32449 of the class C2X, capable of hauling ten times this load. (P. Hay)

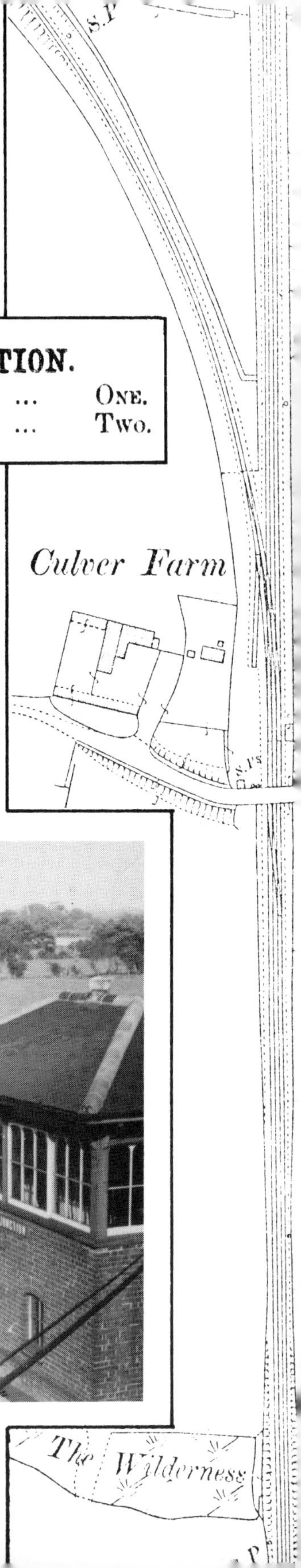

ENGINE WHISTLES.—CULVER JUNCTION.

To or from Uckfield Line	One.
To or from East Grinstead Line	Two.

41. Class E4 0–6–2T no. 32582 slows to give up the single line token on 2nd September 1953. This train was the 3.35 pm Oxted to Brighton service. The direct line to Tunbridge Wells passes through Barcombe Mills station, seen in the distance. (R.C. Riley)

BARCOMBE

42. Until 2nd January 1885 this station was known as New Barcombe, to distinguish it from the station glimpsed in the previous photograph, but it was a further 12 years before goods sidings were provided, the installation costing £1450. (Lens of Sutton)

0354
L. B. & S. C. RY.
This half available for 8 DAYS including DATE of issue and return.
This ticket is issued subject to the Regulations & Conditions stated in the Company's Time Tables & Bills.
E. GRINSTEAD TO
BARCOMBE
Third Cl. 2s. 7d.

2691
L. B. & S. C. RY.
This half available for 8 DAYS including DATE of issue and return.
This Ticket is issued subject to the Regulations & Conditions stated in the Company's Time Tables & Bills.
BRIGHTON to
BARCOMBE
3rd Cl. Revised Fare 3/7

1910 Map.

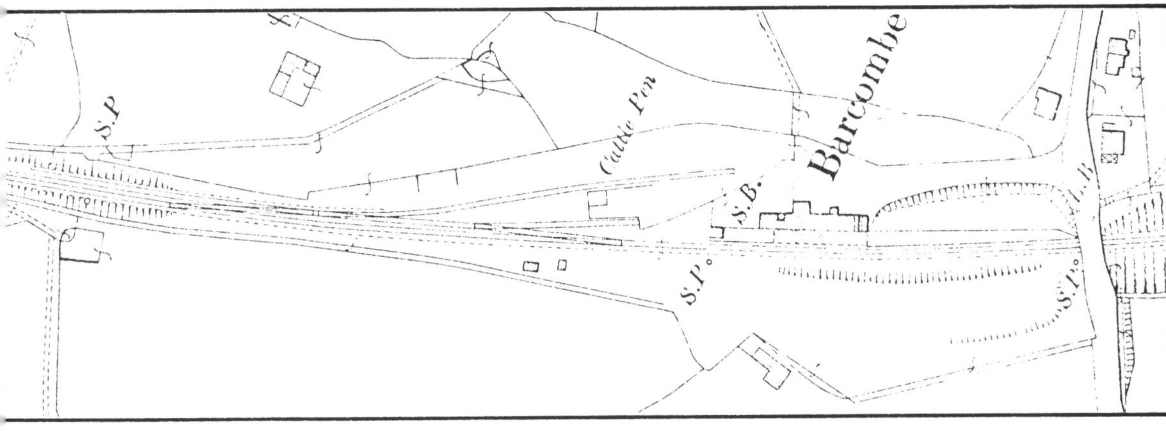

43. B1 or Gladstone Class no. 185 *George A. Wallis* photographed at the south end of the platform with the station approach road behind. This locomotive was built in 1889 and scrapped in 1923. (Lens of Sutton)

44. All the bridges on this line were built to allow for double track, but it was always single between Culver Junction and Horsted Keynes. By the time this photograph was taken on 2nd September 1953, the canopy had been shortened. The obligatory set of fire buckets were well illuminated by a large paraffin bracket lamp. (R.C. Riley)

45. Viewed from the road bridge on the same day we see a class E4 0-6-2T accelerating away with a birdcage set – this was three coaches semi-permanently coupled with look-outs at each end. Examples of all this rolling stock are still to be seen a few miles north, running on the Bluebell Line. (R.C. Riley)

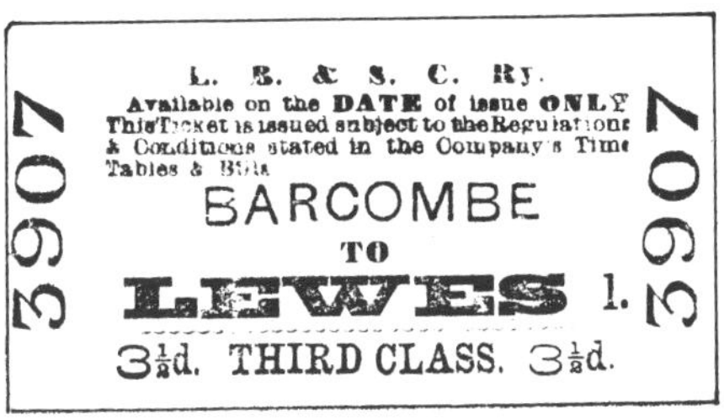

3907
L. B. & S. C. Ry.
Available on the DATE of issue ONLY
This Ticket is issued subject to the Regulations & Conditions stated in the Company's Time Tables & Bills
BARCOMBE
TO
LEWES 1.
3½d. THIRD CLASS. 3½d.
3907

0794
L. B. & S. C. Ry.
TICKET FOR BICYCLE.
When accompanied by passenger.
BARCOMBE
TO ANY STATION ON THE L.B.&S.C.RY.
NOT EXCEEDING 25 MILES
RATE 6d.
This Ticket is available for a single Journey
Only, and must be given up on arrival.
FOR CONDI ONS SEE BACK
0794

46. Station master, four staff and contractors pose at the station prior to its opening in August 1882. The main station building is very similar to Lavant, which is illustrated in our *Branch Lines to Midhurst*. The architectural extravagance went as far as the provision of a refreshment room at this remote location. (R.C. Riley Collection)

47. Under the canopy we can see the enormous stanchions and massive staircase stringer (top right) although there were never many passengers to impress with the air of opulence. Even the glazing had a frosted pattern to add to the general ornamentation. (R.C. Riley Collection)

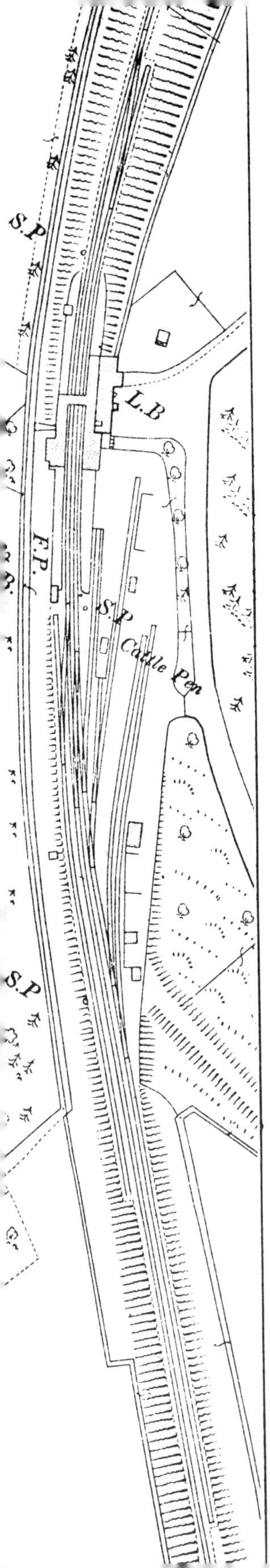

1910 Map.

"KING'S HEAD" INN

CHAILEY.

This pleasantly situated and well-known Inn, offers every facility for

DINNER, TEA AND PICNIC PARTIES

LARGE GROUNDS WELL LAID OUT,

In fact, every convenience that the Visitor may require.

G. NEWTON, Proprietor

48. Looking south in March 1955, the sagging canopy and almost deserted goods yard makes a sorry sight, although the chimney pots and sewer vent pipes were still impressive. (Pamlin Prints)

49. In 1955 the service from East Grinstead to Lewes was withdrawn. Following the legal battle outlined in the introduction to this book, the service was recommenced on 7th August 1956. This photograph shows class K no. 32342 with the first train over the re-opened line, arriving at Newick amidst much celebration. The crowds quickly disappeared and deserted the railway once again. (P. Hay)

50. Class C2X no. 32440 running tender first leaves with the 12.28 pm East Grinstead to Lewes train on 26th August 1956. Notice the sheet tied to the cab to keep out bad weather and flying coal dust. The down platform buildings, the signal box, the loop and the elaborate footbridge had long since gone – white elephants from the start. (S.C. Nash)

SHEFFIELD PARK

51. Originally named Fletching and Sheffield Park, the village name was dropped following objections from the Earl of Sheffield. Local farm workers appear to be demonstrating the art of churn rolling, whilst the station staff make themselves look busy as the stationmaster is present, or was it just for the benefit of the photographer? Notice the architectural similarity to the previous station. (Lens of Sutton)

52. Four staff, plus cycle, pose outside the front door. Again the design is similar to the buildings on the Midhurst to Chichester line, including the decorative plaster work and tile hanging, the latter being added to the stations of both lines some years after their construction. Photo c.1922 (R. Resch Collection)

53. Pictured on 26th April 1931, we see no. B537 (one of the C2X class fitted with an extra dome, to cover the top boiler feed fittings) shunting onto the up line. It is probably being coupled onto a milk van (note the churns on the platform) which will be attached to the front of the Lewes-bound passenger train standing at the down platform. It seems that the guard is about to cross the line to talk to the driver who is half way round the oiling-up of the inside motion of his well-groomed steed. (H.C. Casserley)

A sketch map of 1910 showing the position of the Mid-Sussex Creamery's tramway referred to in the accompanying extract from the LBSCR *Appendix to the Service Timetable*, dated August 1922. (Brighton Circle)

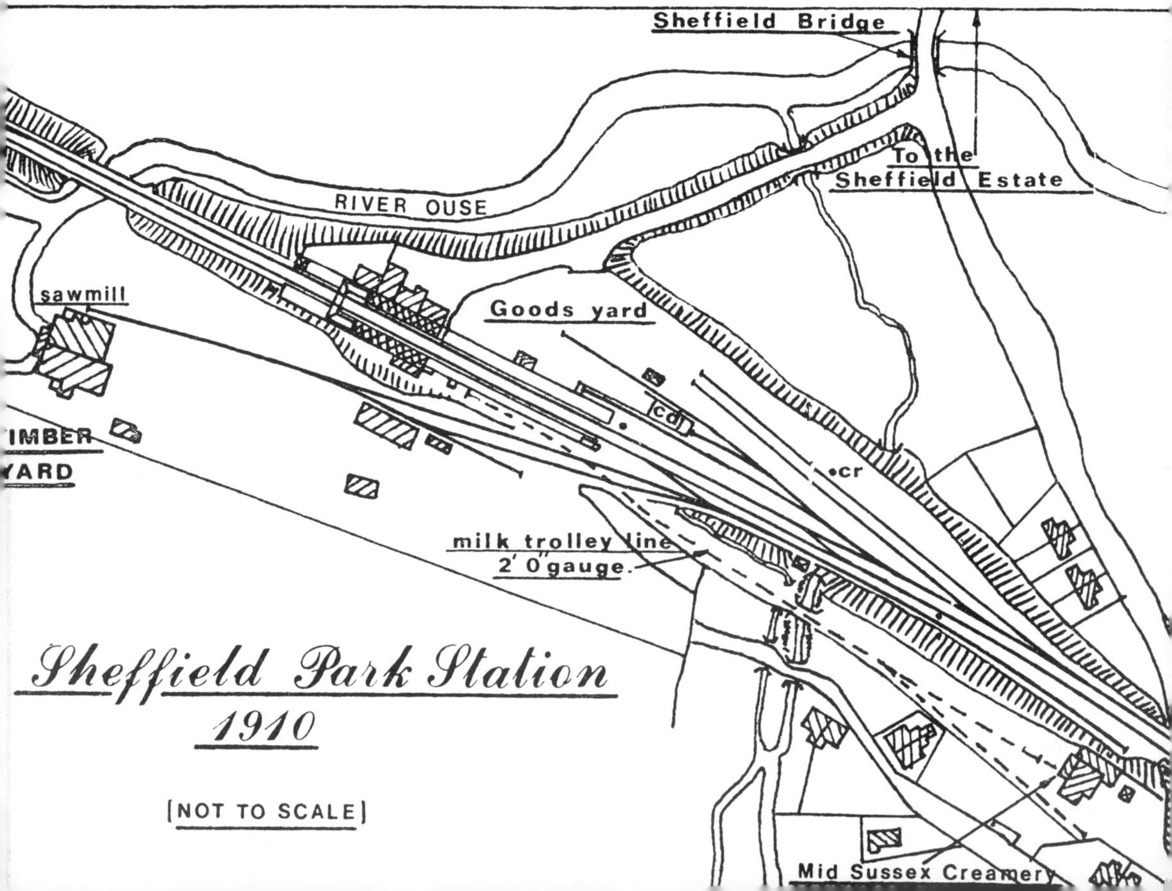

54. The North Box (seen here from the footbridge) and the South Box were abolished and replaced by the present frame on the down platform, which could be operated by a booking clerk/signalman. Similar installations exist today at Falmer and Amberley. The fireman of this E5 tank, pictured here on 25th August 1934, has saved the effort of holding the water crane in position by winding its rope round the boiler handrail. Here we see tricks of the trade and the other side of a birdcage. (H.F. Wheeller)

272

SPECIAL INSTRUCTIONS RESPECTING CERTAIN PLACES—*continued.*

Sheffield Park: Dairy Company's Milk Tram Siding.—This light Railway runs from back of Up platform on the Company's property and crosses the rails at entrance to Messrs. Turner's Timber Yard. When Goods Trains are performing shunting operations in Timber Yard, it will be the duty of the Porter Signalman to warn the Dairy employees of the fact, and they must not use the tram lines whilst such work is in hand.

Sheffield Park: Turner & Son's Timber Yard Siding.—This Timber Yard Siding leads out of the Siding on Up side of Line. Catch Points for coming out of the Siding are provided, and secured by a padlock, the key of which is kept by the Station Master, who will be held responsible for the safe working of the Siding.

55. The locomotive leaves a puddle on the foot crossing whilst the driver waits for a green flag on the penultimate day of passenger services through to Lewes, 15th March 1958. Few could imagine at that time that this station was yet to receive more passengers than at any time in its previous history, becoming the starting point of Britain's first preserved standard gauge passenger railway. The five millionth visitor arrived on 25th September 1983. (J. Scrace)

56. The story of the remarkable growth of the Bluebell Railway is well told in its own publications. The first train ran in 1960 and this view of the south end of the station, taken on 22nd July 1967, is typical of that decade. Massive volunteer effort helped to re-equip every aspect of the railway. Here we see a restored LBSCR milk van on the left, standing in the former timber yard siding; P class tank *Bluebell* taking water in the down platform and no.473 *Birch Grove* at the former cattle dock, then used for coaling. (J. Scrace)

57. The new management erected a small asbestos-clad engine shed which soon proved inadequate. Non-native locomotives soon arrived from various parts of Britain. From the left we see in September 1965 the tender of a GWR Dukedog; a rare geared industrial locomotive by Aveling & Porter; a North London Railway 0–6–0T; an ex-LSWR 4–4–2T and finally a native Terrier. The water tower on the right receives water pumped from the adjacent River Ouse.
(J. Scrace)

58. Some of the remarkable achievements of the Bluebell Railway Preservation Society are to be seen in this photograph taken on 3rd December 1983. The locomotive fleet now numbers 29, of which the rear ends of five are visible. From left to right – no. 55 *Stepney*, no. 21C123 *Blackmore Vale*, Q class no. 541, ex BR class 9F no. 92240 and a Schools class no. 928 *Stowe*. Other commendable features to note are the scissors crossover, the new 3-road locomotive shed and the spacious workshop building.
(V. Mitchell)

59. The Bluebell Railway opened a new halt on 1st April 1962 and named it Holywell (Waterworks). It was short lived owing to problems with the planning authority. Here we see *Primrose* hauling the *Wealden Rambler*, comprised of ex-Metropolitan Railway coaches last used on the Chesham branch in Buckinghamshire hence the description – the Chesham set. (R.C. Riley)

←

60. P class 0–6–0T no. 27, restored to its impressive SECR livery with the 3.25 pm Horsted Keynes to Sheffield Park train, near Holywell in April 1969. The photograph also shows the ex-LNWR double ended observa--tion car, preserved by the Bluebell Railway. This is the only pre-grouping observation car still in existence and between 1978 and 1982 a major overhaul was undertaken, mainly by volunteers. Another halt was opened at Freshfield and is still in use today, mainly for the benefit of walkers. (J. Scrace)

SOUTHERN RY
Available on the DATE of issue ONLY.
This ticket is issued subject to the Regulations & Conditions stated in the Company's Time Tables & Bills.
SHEFFIELD PARK
TO
EAST GRINSTEAD e.g
THIRD CLASS.
1/4 Fare 1/4
6882
6882

BRITISH RAILWAYS (S)
SHEFFIELD PARK
PLATFORM TICKET 1d.
Available ONE HOUR on Day of Issue only.
NOT VALID IN TRAINS. NOT TRANSFERABLE.
To be given up when leaving Platform.
FOR CONDITIONS SEE BACK.
1 2 3 4 5 6
4625
4625

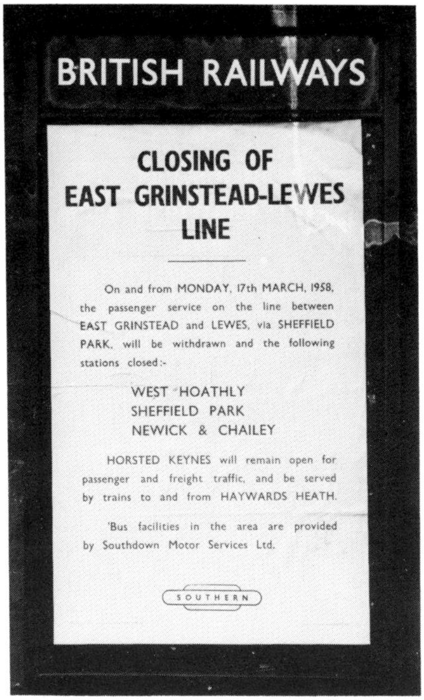

BRITISH RAILWAYS
CLOSING OF
EAST GRINSTEAD-LEWES
LINE
On and from MONDAY, 17th MARCH, 1958, the passenger service on the line between EAST GRINSTEAD and LEWES, via SHEFFIELD PARK, will be withdrawn and the following stations closed:-
WEST HOATHLY
SHEFFIELD PARK
NEWICK & CHAILEY
HORSTED KEYNES will remain open for passenger and freight traffic, and be served by trains to and from HAYWARDS HEATH.
'Bus facilities in the area are provided by Southdown Motor Services Ltd.
SOUTHERN

61. When the Bluebell commenced operations, trains terminated at a temporary halt by a road bridge, about ¼ mile south of Horsted Keynes. Beyond the train, a fence across the track can be seen which marked the company's boundary. Later a BR pilotman accompanied trains from this point into the station. Eventually it all became Bluebell property. (R.C. Riley)

HORSTED KEYNES

62. Navvies and a family, but not the station staff, appear in this pre-opening photograph. The left hand island platform was provided for trains to and from Haywards Heath. The ornate panelling was later tile hung (see photo no.64). (Lens of Sutton)

63. The three sidings to the west of the station were often used for the storage of locomotives awaiting scrapping or entry to Brighton Locomotive Works for overhaul. This view from the signal box was taken about 1906. (Lens of Sutton)

64. No. 2284 was one of the Southern Railway's 0–4–2 tanks of class DI, quite adequate for a 2-coach Lewes train on 3rd March 1934. Like the locomotive, the tapered signal posts were of LBSCR origin. The water crane beyond bore a notice which read *Water only to be taken by enginemen when absolutely necessary*. The canopy stanchion brackets make interesting comparison – wood and cast iron.
(H.C. Casserley)

65. The double track to the right joined the main London to Brighton main line north of Haywards Heath. There was one intermediate station at Ardingly. After electrification on 7th July 1935, it ceased to carry many through trains, other than in emergency. The single line to Culver Junction commenced in the centre distance. Photo date – 8.3.58.
(Pamlin Prints)

66. The interior of the box in September 1950, with Bill Moon on duty. It was manned day and night during World War II on account of its important position on a diversionary route. (R.C. Riley)

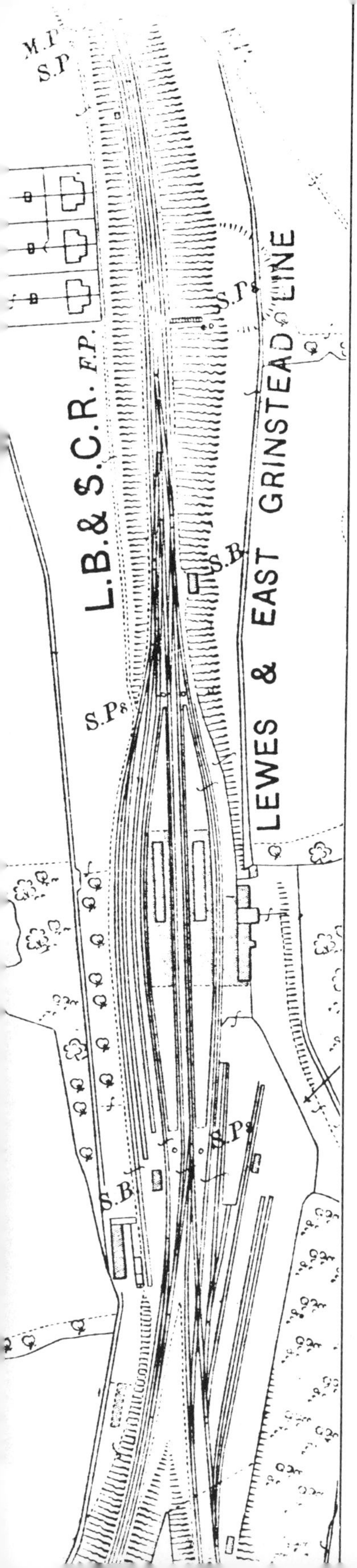

Map 1910.

3rd - SINGLE SINGLE - 3rd
0519
Horsted Keynes to
Horsted Keynes
West Hoathly
Horsted Keynes
West Hoathly
WEST HOATHLY
(S) 6d.H FARE 6d.H (S)
For conditions see over For conditions see over
0519

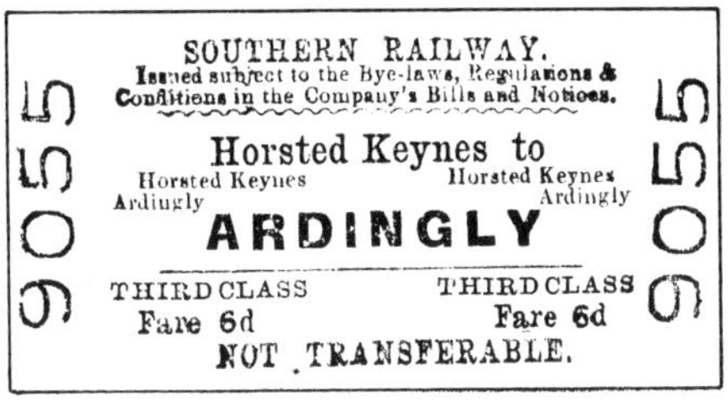

SOUTHERN RAILWAY.
Issued subject to the Bye-laws, Regulations & Conditions in the Company's Bills and Notices.
9055
Horsted Keynes to
Horsted Keynes
Ardingly
Horsted Keynes
Ardingly
ARDINGLY
THIRD CLASS
Fare 6d
THIRD CLASS
Fare 6d
NOT TRANSFERABLE.
9055

67. Ivatt 2–6–2T no. 41318 leaving with the 4.03 pm (Saturdays only) Lewes to East Croydon train on 16th April 1955. On Monday to Friday this train formed the 4.55 pm Horsted Keynes to Brighton (see picture 45). This class, originally built by the LMS in 1946, was continued by BR until 1952 for branch line work. The nearest platform (originally up main) and the two adjacent sidings lost their rails in World War I. (S.C. Nash)

68. K class no. 32342 with a rambler's excursion on Sunday 11th May 1958. The train had been worked from Greenford to East Croydon by GWR 4-4-0 *City of Truro*, which spent the day on Norwood Junction Shed, which had specially groomed 32342. These excursions were popular in the 1950s and added interest to the railway scene. Notice that the starting signals have been modernised. (J. Scrace)

70 It seemed curious that the platform which had the most frequent train service, and the only one that had the third rail, had no passenger shelter whatsoever. Plans have been announced to replace the canopy, using one removed from Lavant station. Just leaving is a 2BIL unit on the 2.16 pm service to Seaford, via Haywards Heath and Lewes, on 27th October 1962, whilst a Bluebell locomotive blows off in the background. The line to Haywards Heath was closed on 28th October 1963, but BR still transports road stone from Somerset to a private terminal at Ardingly. (S.C. Nash)

←

69. We see here, from the top of the water tower, the first Bluebell Railway train to depart from this station. It was on 29th September 1961, the last day of the operating season. (R.C. Riley)

2nd-SINGLE SINGLE-2nd
0009
Horsted Keynes to
Sheffield Park
Sheffield Park
SHEFFIELD PARK
Via Direct
FARE
0009

WEST HOATHLY

71. This is a northward view from above the portal of Sharpthorne Tunnel (a notoriously wet tunnel), which was 730 yds long and pierced the ridge of the Hastings Beds. The nearby villagers had the luxury of a fully glazed footbridge when taking an occasional trip to market. Beyond it can be seen the tiny goods shed. (Lens of Sutton)

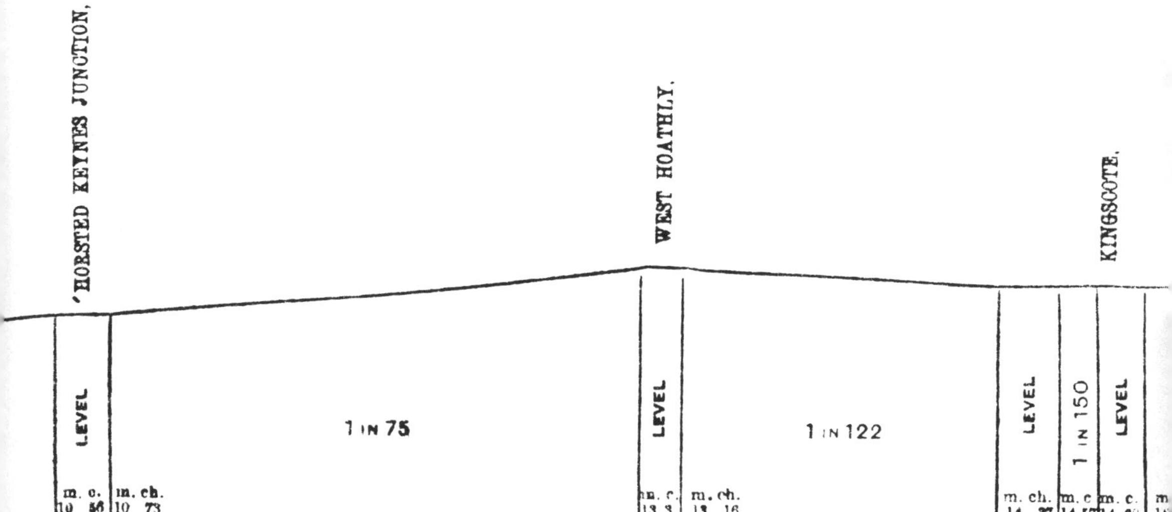

72. As this K class locomotive gains momentum with the 3.28 pm Haywards Heath to London Bridge train in April 1955, we have another chance to look at the goods shed and *through* a bird cage. (P. Hay)

73. A sad and unique chapter in the history of the railways of Britain and probably the world, was the running of the so-called *spite service* during the enforced reopening of the line. Many wanted it; few used it; the taxpayers paid for it; a large locomotive pulled a single coach and the train crews yawned with boredom. (R.C. Riley)

74. Notice on the goods shed door in 1954. Wagon doors were propped up at all other stations – perhaps the signs had "gone missing" elsewhere. (J.H. Aston)

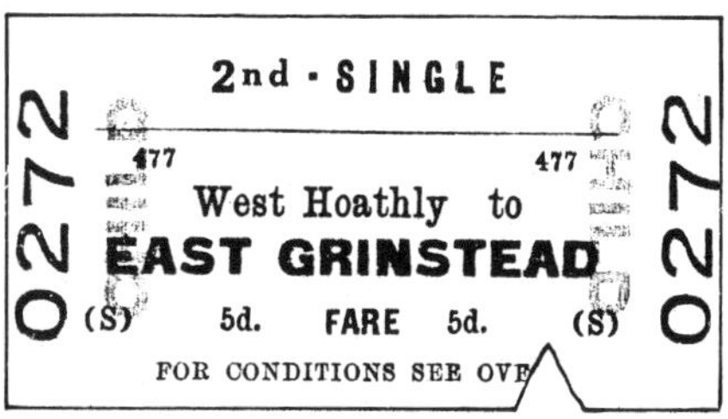

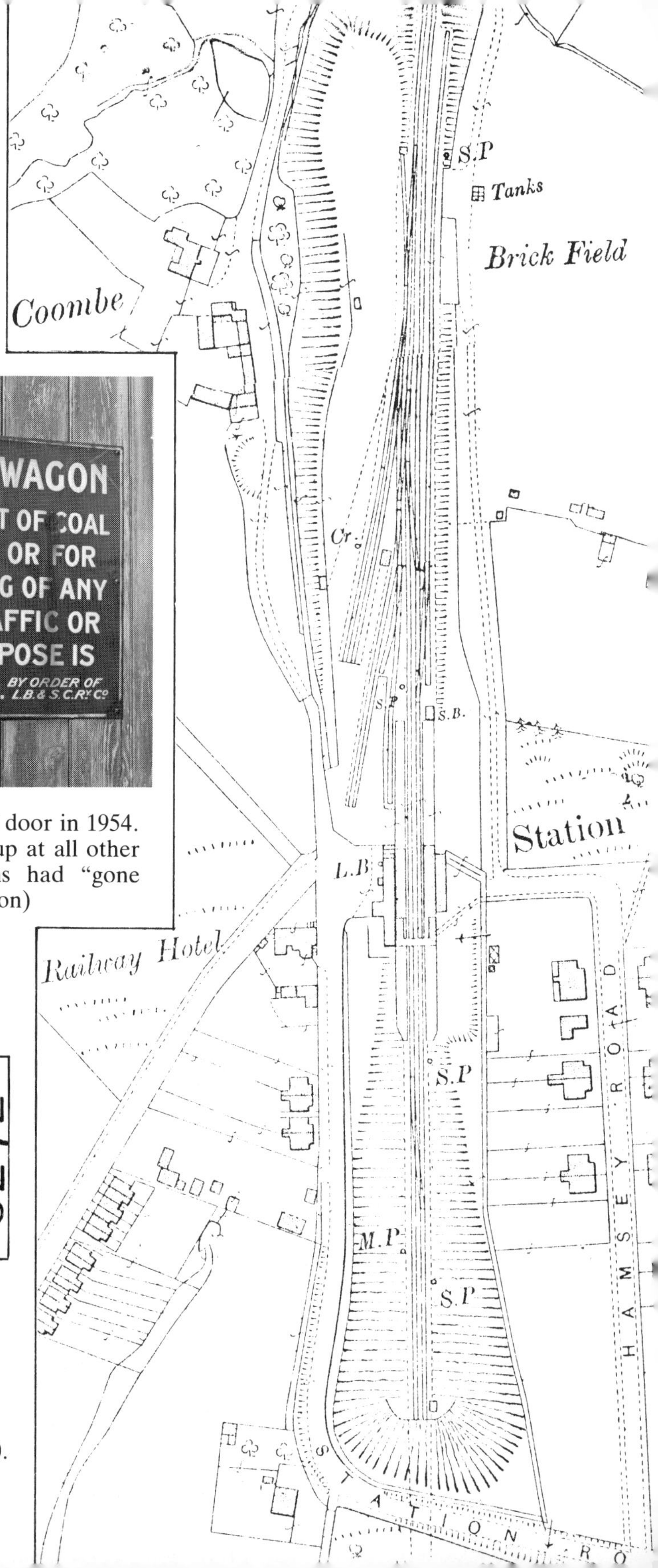

Map 1910.

75. The impressive massive dimensions can detract from interesting details – the built-in letter box (marked LB on the map), the built-in foot scraper, the king-size paraffin lamp which gave twilight candlepower (only Horsted Keynes on this line was electrically lit), the footbridge roof and the station master's curtains still drawn together although the sun is well up. (P. Hay)

76. During track lifting operations in 1964-65, the contractors hired a locomotive (ex-North London Railway 0–6–0T) from the Bluebell Railway. It was driven and fired by Jack Owen, still on the Bluebell staff today, and returned from East Grinstead by road on a low-loader. (R.C. Riley)

KINGSCOTE

77. This station was as substantial as the others on the line (but with taller chimney pots) and was even more remote from habitation. Looking south, we see the former cattle dock and a SR upper quadrant signal (with the post made from two old rails) and in the distance an LBSCR lower quadrant, on a wooden post.
(H.S. Brighty/R.C. Riley Collection)

78. The end is nigh. In January 1965 little is left, although the subway railings are still standing. Like Barcombe, trains did not stop here during the *sulky service* period. Although both stations were opened right from the start, they were not mentioned in the original Act of Parliament. (E. Wilmshurst)

Map 1910.

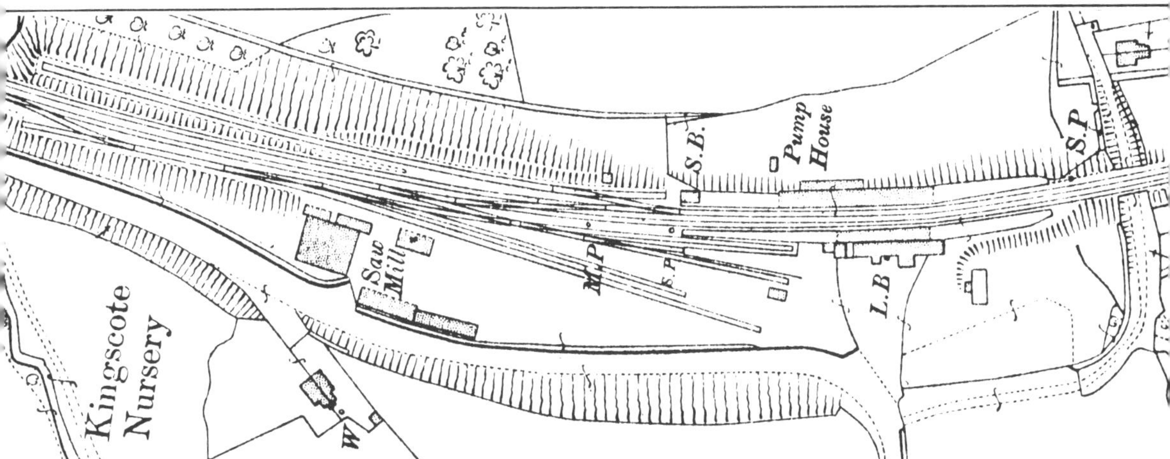

79. The viaduct is less than ½ mile south of East Grinstead station and still carries track which permits shunting into the former low-level goods yard. Imberhorne Manor occupied much of the land to the west of the town until recent times and between 1884 and 1948 had its own private siding on the Three Bridges line. (R.C. Riley)

80. Just coming off the ten arched viaduct, we see class C2X 0–6–0 no. 32521 with a single coach (ex-LBSCR motor set), about to enter East Grinstead low level station, in December 1957. (P. Hay)

Tunbridge Wells towards East Grinstead

TUNBRIDGE WELLS WEST

81 The suffix WEST was added by the Southern Railway on 22nd August 1923, to distinguish it from the former SER station which was named CENTRAL. The last quarter of the 19th century saw a series of improvements and enlargements to the station. The imposing building, complete with a clock tower, is now a listed structure and retains a gas-lit booking hall with an elaborate ornamental ceiling.
(R.M. Newan/E.R. Lacey Collection)

82. The first locomotive shed was on the south side of the station and was replaced by this larger 4-road shed to the north-west in 1891. D class tank no. 272 had been built in 1880, named *Nevill* and re-named *Goring* in 1897, being withdrawn in 1925. (E.R. Lacey Collection)

84. A smart D3 waits outside the goods shed in 1921. One of the approach roads to the goods yard can be seen crossing the sidings on the right of the picture. This necessitated special safety precautions. The shed is now used by a wholesale fruiterer and the yard serves as stabling for up to 20 DEMUs at night. (B.C. Vigor)

85. The signal box by Montacute Road Bridge has been variously named – East Cabin, No. 2 Box and B Box. The semaphore in the off position has been replaced by a colour light. (J. Scrace)

83. On 11th March 1905, class C1 no. 425 ran into the turntable pit at the same time as Stroudley's 2–2–2 no. 342 *St. Lawrence* was being turned. There was damage to the brake gear and framing and before recovery, its chimney was removed. On the last day of the same year the locomotive left the road again, when it ran off the end of a siding at Eridge. (J. Scrace Collection)

86. The train is the empty stock of the 12.20 pm (Saturdays only) arrival from London Bridge on 16th March 1957. The stock consists of five of the then relatively modern BR standard compartment coaches, with a former LSWR composite coach sandwiched near the middle. Behind the C class locomotive is the engine shed, the roof of which was replaced with corrugated asbestos following bomb damage in World War II. (R.C. Riley)

88. The A Box has 33 levers and was formerly known as Tunbridge Wells West *West*. Although there is now only an hourly through service, both boxes are fully staffed to permit the shunting of empty stock. Little has changed since this photograph was taken in 1969. (J. Scrace)

87. Here we see from the road bridge in 1958 (from left to right), the goods yard and shed, carriage sidings, down platform canopy, locomotive shed roof, main station buildings with clock tower, No. 2 bay and the dock. (J. Scrace)

HIGH ROCKS HALT

89. The halt was opened on 1st June 1907 when the *Motor Trains* were introduced and was situated in a very thinly populated area. It seems to have been mainly used by urban dwellers wishing to visit the splendid countryside in this vicinity, a notable feature of which is the rocky outcrops of the central Wealden sandstone. This was the roadside sign that must have given relief to many returning hikers (Lens of Sutton)

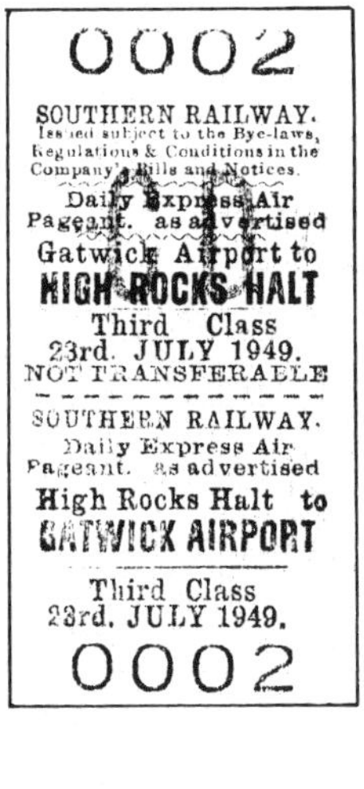

0002

SOUTHERN RAILWAY.
Issued subject to the Bye-laws, Regulations & Conditions in the Company's Bills and Notices.
Daily Express Air Pageant. as advertised
Gatwick Airport to
HIGH ROCKS HALT
Third Class
23rd. JULY 1949.
NOT TRANSFERABLE

SOUTHERN RAILWAY.
Daily Express Air Pageant. as advertised
High Rocks Halt to
GATWICK AIRPORT
Third Class
23rd. JULY 1949.

0002

90. A former Southern Railway Q class no. 30546 darkens the countryside as it clanks past the battered corrugated iron shelter and the chipped enamel WAY OUT sign, with a train from Tunbridge Wells West. (Lens of Sutton)

91. The up platform is in the foreground, on the edge of Broadwater Forest, its counterpart being in the distance, on the other side of the bridge. The halt was finally closed on the 5th May 1952, although it was temporarily shut during the 1939-42 period. The shelters are made from similar materials to all the stations featured in our *Branch Line to Selsey*. (Lens of Sutton)

GROOMBRIDGE

92. An early faded postcard shows the spacious staggered platforms with very generous canopies for such a rural station. It was used as a junction for north-south travellers for many years, with Eastbourne coaches being detached from London trains from 1888 until 1914. (E. Jackson Collection)

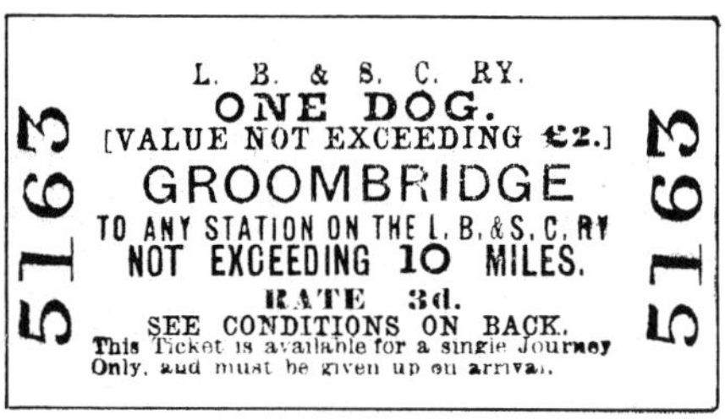
5163
L. B. & S. C. RY.
ONE DOG.
[VALUE NOT EXCEEDING £2.]
GROOMBRIDGE
TO ANY STATION ON THE L. B. & S. C. RY
NOT EXCEEDING 10 MILES.
RATE 3d.
SEE CONDITIONS ON BACK.
This Ticket is available for a single Journey Only, and must be given up on arrival.
5163

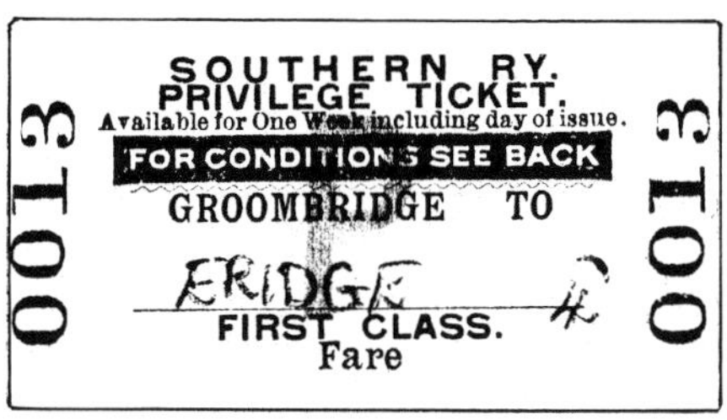
0013
SOUTHERN RY.
PRIVILEGE TICKET.
Available for One Week including day of issue.
FOR CONDITIONS SEE BACK
GROOMBRIDGE TO
ERIDGE
FIRST CLASS.
Fare
0013

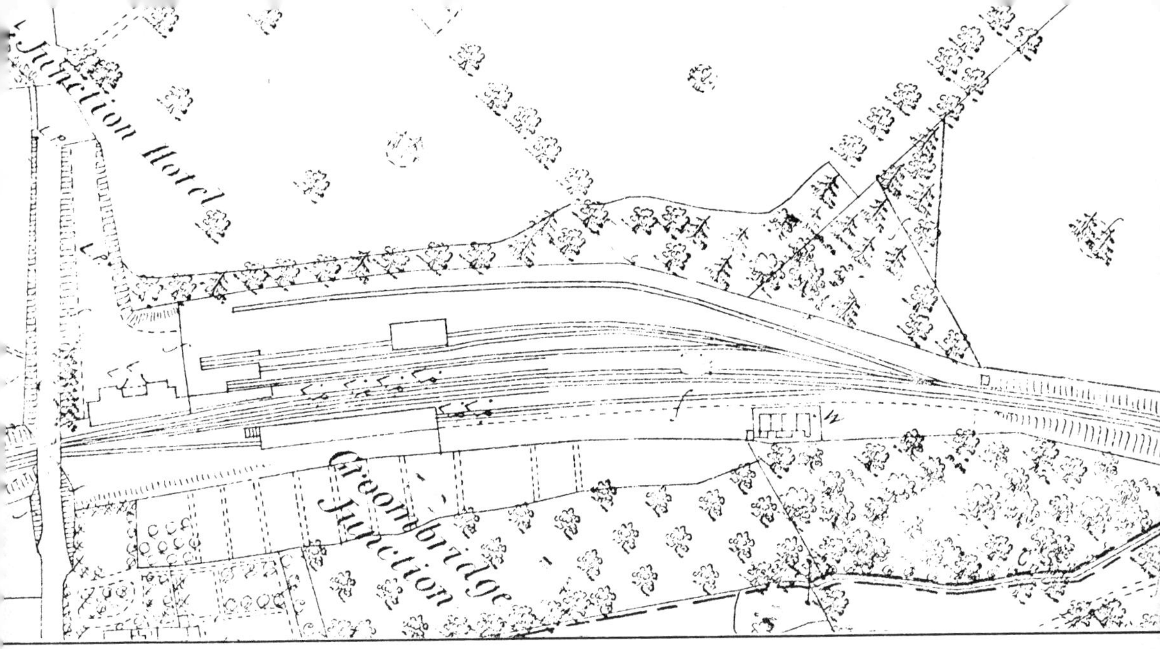

The 1874 map, with LP showing the position of every lamp post.

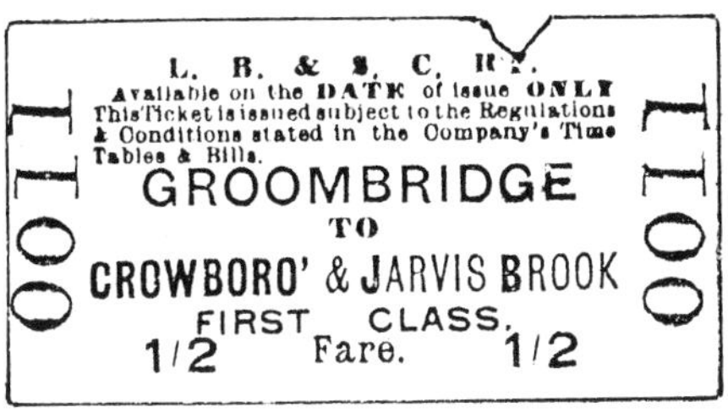

93. This unusual LBSCR signal box was at the north end of the station, until replaced by a flat-roofed affair in the 1950s. A separate box was provided for Groombridge Junction, nearly ½ mile to the south.
(R.C. Riley/Lens of Sutton)

94. The predominance of round-headed windows gives an impression of a LSWR station but the small tower is a reminder of its neighbour to the east. Built in 1866, it was largely rebuilt in 1897 and pictured here in 1961. (R.M. Casserley)

95. Shorn of its shelters, we see the subway with covered steps, the rail-less goods shed, and the now abandoned signal box of relatively modern construction. A diesel-electric 3-coach set throbs in the down platform in August 1976, ready to leave for Eridge. (J. Scrace)

96. The driver of the 2.08 pm Three Bridges to Tunbridge Wells West train on 19th July 1958, gives up the token for the single line at Ashurst Junction which can be seen in the distance. His H class tank appears to have been coaled up by a bricklayer. The signal box was built in 1914 and had 35 levers. (E. Wilmshurst)

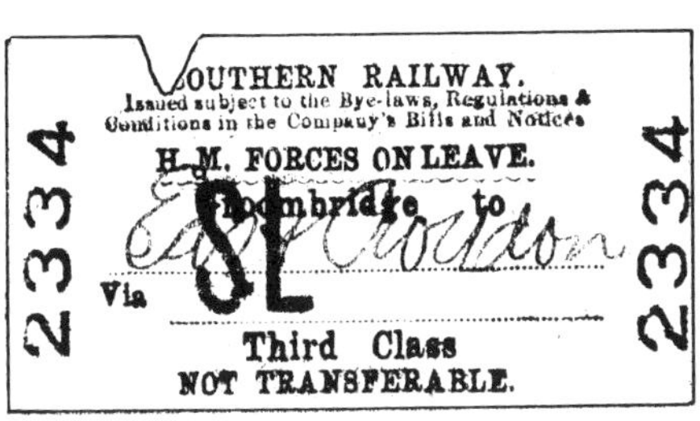

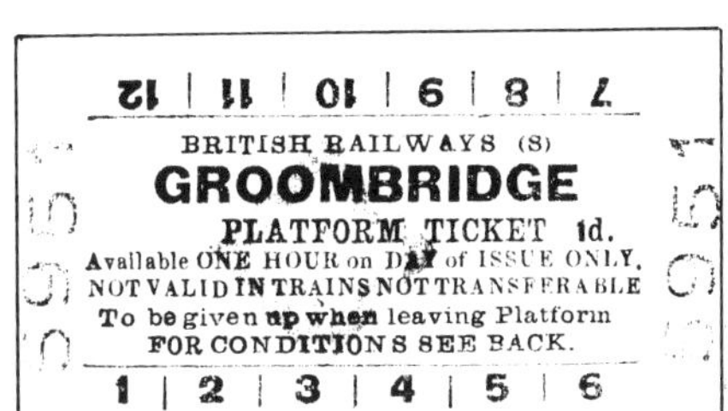

WITHYHAM

97. An eastbound train plods placidly away leaving this unchanged country station to another prolonged period of peace. The flame seen in the level crossing lamp will have no cause to flicker. Oh, glorious past! (Pamlin Prints)

London Brighton & South Coast Railway.

Hartfield to

Withyham

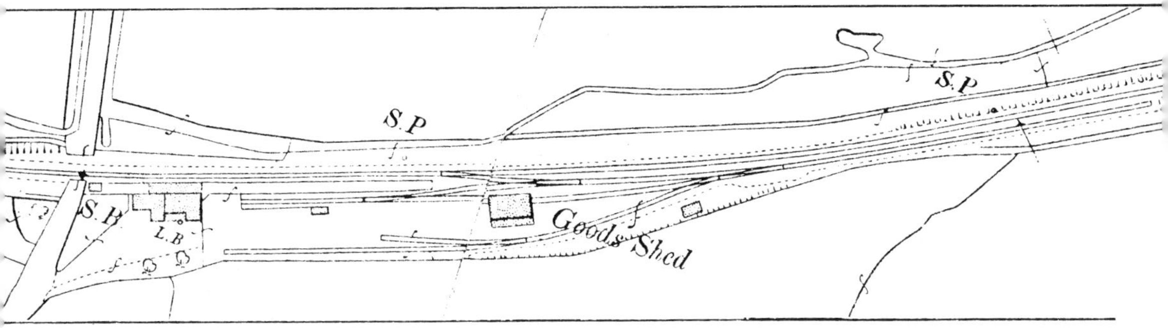

Map dated 1910.

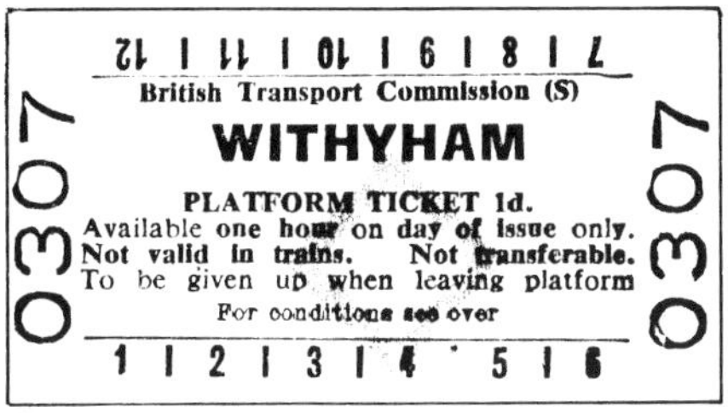

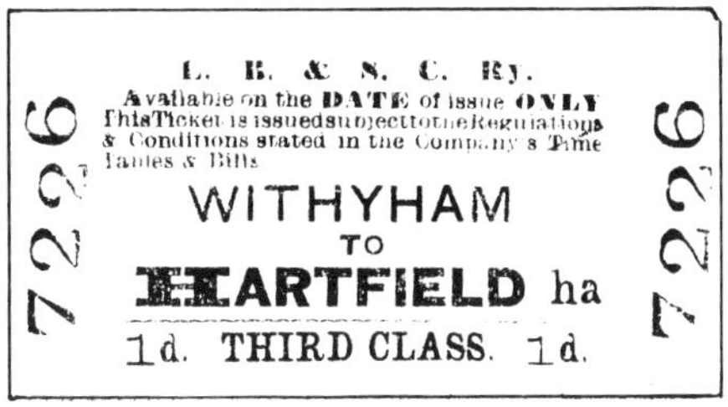

98. A modeller's paradise. Simple hipped slate roofs and a minimal goods yard. The intricate barge boards and valances might be overlooked. The signal box in the distance has been preserved privately, elsewhere in Sussex. (Lens of Sutton)

HARTFIELD

99. This local postcard shows the signal box in the distance. Across the field on the left were the upper reaches of the River Medway and the field to the south was Castle Field, although only a mound remained in it. In the early years, almost all local commercial traffic passed through the station, necessitating a staff of three. (Lens of Sutton)

The 1910 map showing a goods yard loop that could hold 13 wagons.

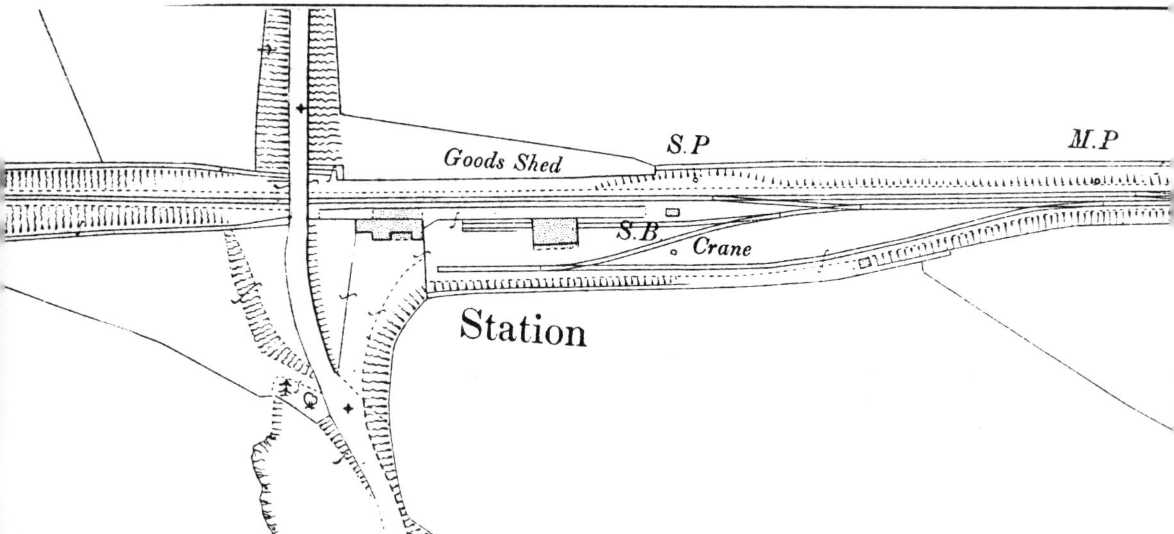

100. A glimpse under the road bridge in 1953 reveals a similar scene to that which we saw from Withyham level crossing, although here the goods shed is visible. (E. Wilmshurst)

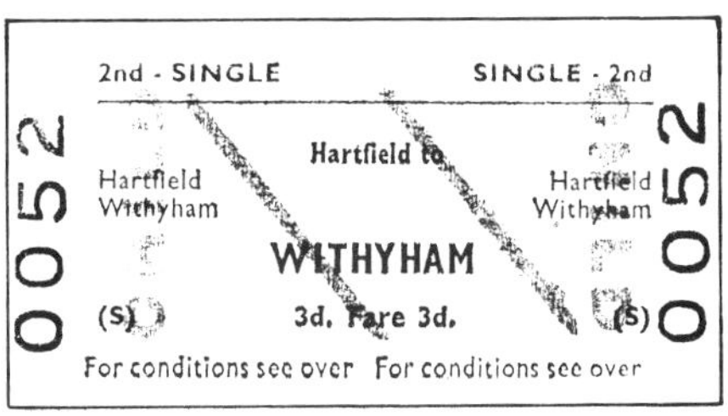

0052
2nd - SINGLE SINGLE - 2nd
Hartfield to
Hartfield Withyham
Hartfield Withyham
WITHYHAM
(S) 3d. Fare 3d. (S)
For conditions see over For conditions see over
0052

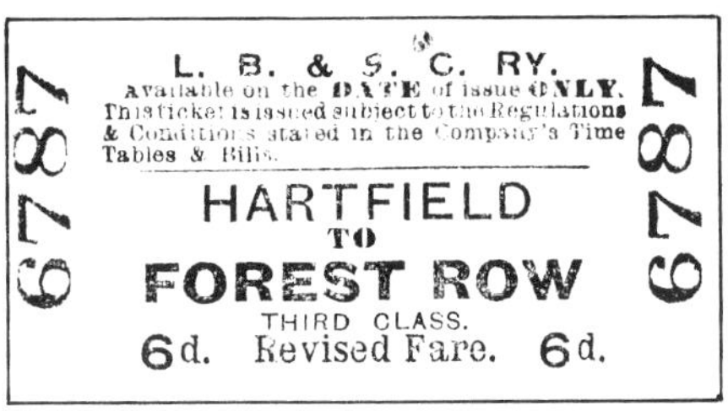

6787
L. B. & S. C. RY.
Available on the DATE of issue ONLY.
This ticket is issued subject to the Regulations & Conditions stated in the Company's Time Tables & Bills.
HARTFIELD
TO
FOREST ROW
THIRD CLASS.
6d. Revised Fare. 6d.
6787

FOREST ROW

101. This K class 2-6-0 ran out of control descending Brambletye bank with a Three Bridges to Buxted engineer's train on 3rd March 1954 and was derailed at the end of the sand drag. The line was cleared during the night but the locomotive was not recovered until the 7th March, the day after this photograph had been taken. (S.C. Nash)

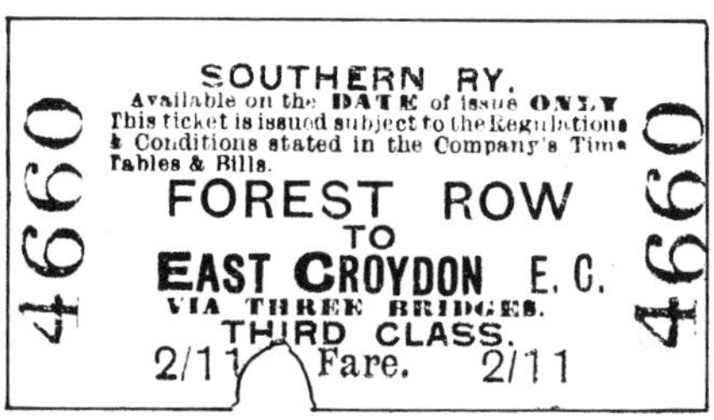

102. A westbound freight hauled by class C2X no. 32536 clatters past the LBSCR pattern starting signals in July 1958. The chimneys are of the pleasing style seen on the previous two stations. (P. Hay)

103. This was the busiest of the intermediate stations and in the final years of the line handled a substantial number of daily travellers to London, as housing development had occurred around the old village. Some trains were extended from East Grinstead to terminate here. The loop, down platform and footbridge date from 1897 and are seen here five years before closure. There was a siding into the goods shed, seen on left, and one other to the south. (H.C. Casserley)

East Grinstead

104. The first station was the terminus of the branch from Three Bridges and was well situated for the town centre, close to London Road. This is the only picture known of the complete station and has suffered from poor storage. The station house survives today, although much modified in 1982. (East Grinstead Town Museum)

106. The first station (in the background) was later used as a dwelling and the tracks used as a goods yard. The company's delivery vehicles are standing outside the second goods shed, a brick built one replacing the original timber structure (N. Stephanakis Collection)

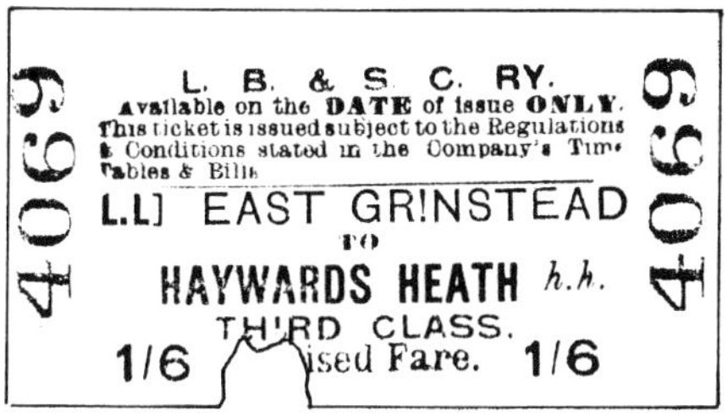

4069
L. B. & S. C. RY.
Available on the DATE of issue ONLY.
This ticket is issued subject to the Regulations
& Conditions stated in the Company's Time
Tables & Bills
L.L] EAST GRINSTEAD
TO
HAYWARDS HEATH h.h.
THIRD CLASS.
1/6 ised Fare. 1/6
4069

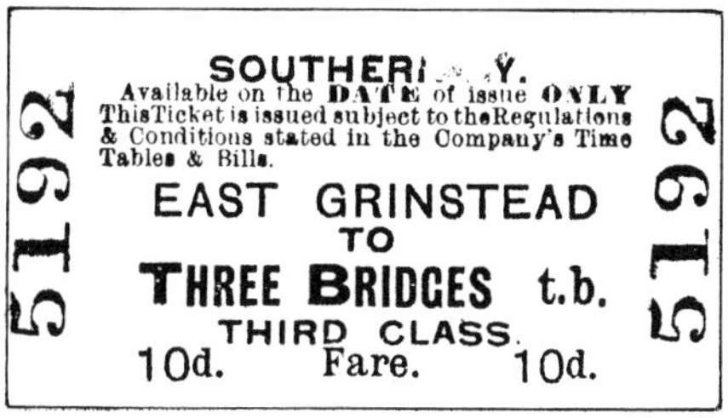

5192
Available on the DATE of issue ONLY
This Ticket is issued subject to the Regulations
& Conditions stated in the Company's Time
Tables & Bills.
EAST GRINSTEAD
TO
THREE BRIDGES t.b.
THIRD CLASS.
10d. Fare. 10d.
5192

105. The second station was opened in 1866 when the line was extended to Tunbridge Wells. It was to the north of the original and at a lower level so that the line could pass under London Road. The waiting room/ entrance hall, booking office and ladies room were at street level, the gents being provided underneath, on both platforms. The entire structure was sold for scrap for £15 in 1907. (East Grinstead Society Collection)

The 1931 map shows the railway system at its zenith. Notice that Station Road passed under the high level platforms and that Railway Approach passed under the line connecting the upper yard, handling mostly goods, and the lower yard, used mainly for coal traffic. The private siding into Stennings timber yard is clearly shown but their 2ft. gauge railway system is omitted.

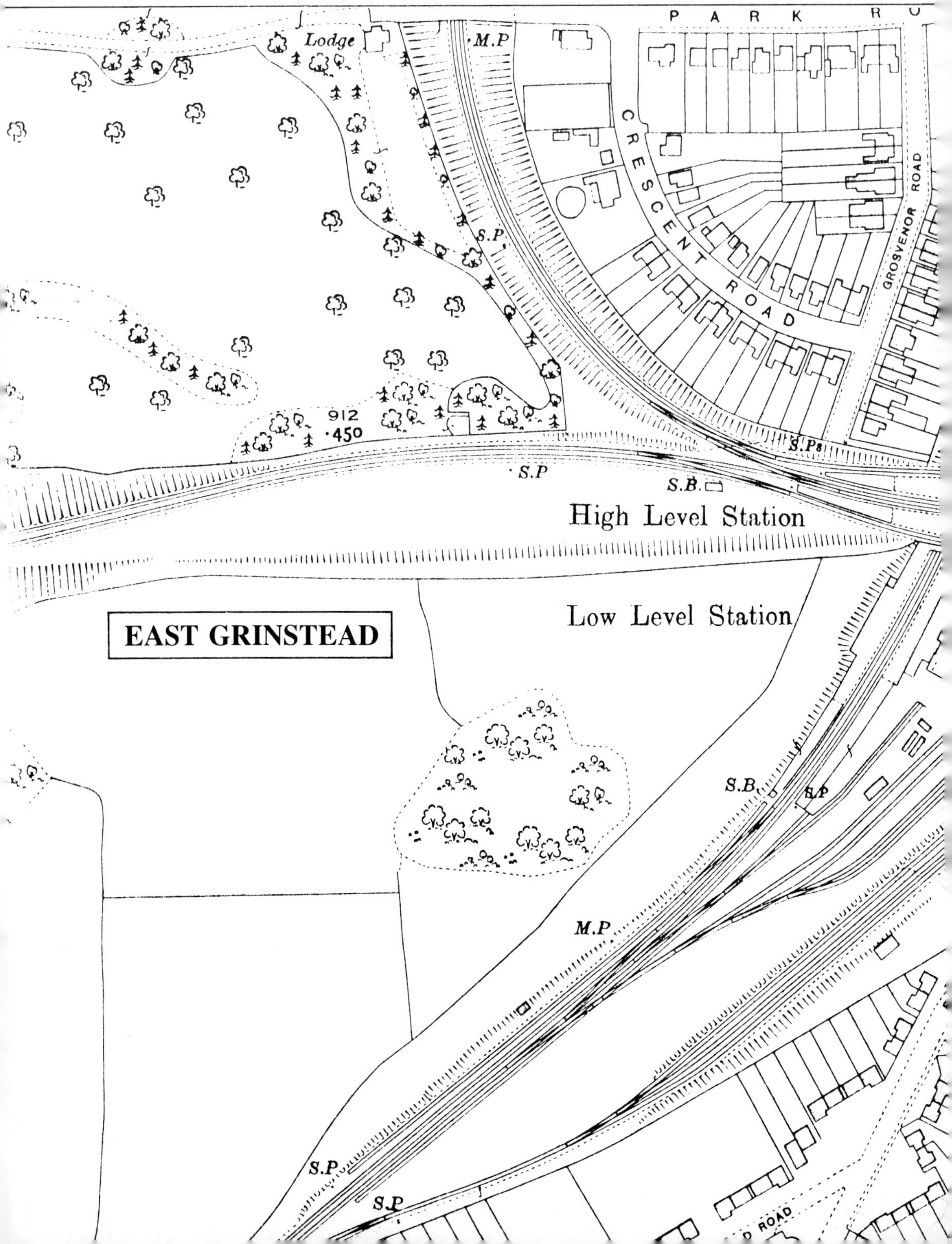

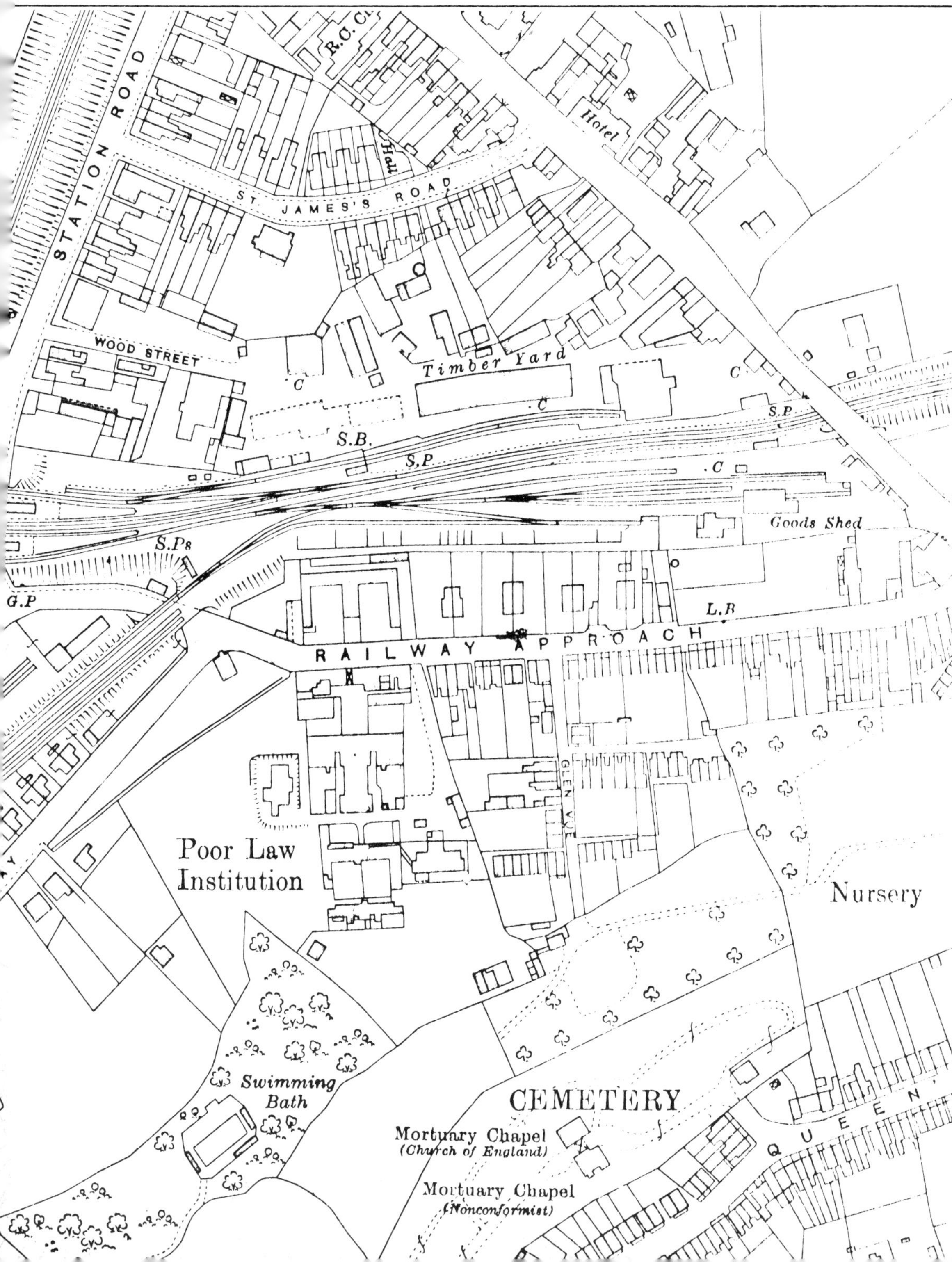
STATION ROAD
R.C. Ch
Hotel
Hall
ST JAMES'S ROAD
WOOD STREET
Timber Yard
C
S.B.
S.P
Goods Shed
S.Ps
G.P
L.B
RAILWAY APPROACH
GLEN VUE
Poor Law
Institution
Nursery
Swimming
Bath
CEMETERY
Mortuary Chapel
(Church of England)
Mortuary Chapel
(Nonconformist)
QUEEN

East Grinstead: Propelling of Goods Train from St. Margaret's Junction to High Level.—Th 12.26 p.m. Kingscote to East Grinstead Goods Train may be propelled from St. Margaret's Junction to the High Lev Station subject to the following precautions being observed:—

The working must be arranged by the Station Master or Person in Charge, who must appoint one of the Station Sta to join the Train at the Low Level and accompany it to the High Level, riding in the leading brake van from St. Margaret Junction.

The Train must not be allowed to leave St. Margaret's Junction until the Block Regulations have been complied wi and all Signals lowered for the Train to proceed as far as East Grinstead East Down Oxted Loop Starting Signal, whe the Train must always be brought to a stand before being allowed on to the Single Line.

East Grinstead: Stenning & Coy's Timber Siding—Siding is situated on the North Side of the High Leve Station and is controlled by the East Box.

Care must be exercised in shunting the Siding and occupying the Single Line, the latter being on a sharply fallin gradient.

Extract from the appendix to the service timetable for August 1922.

107. A third station was necessary when the line from Lewes was opened on 1st August 1882. It was about 300 yards west of its predecessor which remained open for a further 15 months, partly because the two-level exchange station was incomplete and partly due to pressure from local residents who found it less convenient for the town centre. This postcard view shows the substantial nature of the buildings in general and the ventilators over the gentlemen's toilets on the right in particular. (Lens of Sutton)

108. Looking west from the high-level platform on 19th July 1930, we see the single line to Three Bridges beyond the signal box and the double track connection to St. Margaret's Junction on the Oxted line curving away sharply to the right. The locomotive by the water tower (installed in 1920) is B241 and in the centre is B558. (H.C. Casserley)

J. C. Stenning 7 July 1855

EAST GRINSTEAD RAILWAY.

THE LINE

WILL BE OPENED

On MONDAY, the 9th day of JULY.

A SPECIAL TRAIN will leave the Three Bridges Station at One o'Clock for East Grinstead. A SPECIAL TRAIN will also leave East Grinstead at a quarter past Twelve to reach the Three Bridges in time to return by the above Train. You are invited by the Directors to meet either of those Trains.

This Ticket must be produced on entering a Train, and at the Luncheon at Two o'Clock, at East Grinstead, but not delivered up.

WILLIAM PEARLESS,
ARTHUR HASTIE, } SECRETARIES.

109. Ex-SECR Class BI 4-4-0 no. 1101 stands in the low level station on the last day of 1938. The high level platforms can be seen in the background. Refreshment Rooms were provided at both levels. (T. Middlemass)

110. The driver in the leading compartment enjoys peace and quiet as his two-coach train is propelled onto the single line for Three Bridges on 14th April 1951. The line in the foreground is a siding that gives the impression here, and on the map, of double track. The spare land behind the signal box was the course of the railway before the reconstruction of the station. (Pamlin Prints)

111. No. 32547 shunts empty stock past South Box after working a goods service from Norwood Junction on 9th June 1954. In front of the locomotive is the spur into the lower yard. (R.C. Riley)

London Brighton & South Coast Railway.

Dormans to

EAST GRINSTEAD

112. Class E4 no. 32508 coming down the single line connection between the upper and lower yards in December 1957. We cannot explain why the bridge over Railway Approach was built for three tracks as it was never necessary to run regular passenger trains over this spur. The two empty spans only carried the extremities of two sidings (see map). (P. Hay)

6975
L. B. & S. C. RY.
This half available for 2 DAYS including Date of issue and return.
This ticket is issued subject to the Regulations & Conditions stated in the Company's Time Tables & Bills.
Three Bridges to
E.GRINST'AD[H L
Third Cl. 1s. 1d.

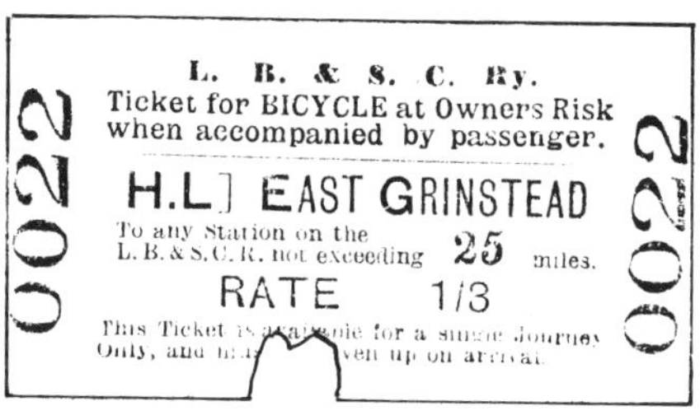

0022
L. B. & S. C. Ry.
Ticket for BICYCLE at Owners Risk when accompanied by passenger.
H.L] EAST GRINSTEAD
To any Station on the L. B. & S. C. R. not exceeding 25 miles.
RATE 1/3
0022

1515
L. B. & S. C. Ry.
Available on the DATE of issue ONLY.
This Ticket is issued subject to the Regulations & Conditions stated in the Company's Time Tables & Bills.
E. GRINSTEAD [H. L.
TO
NORWOOD JUNC'N & SOUTH NORWOOD
Via THREE BRIDGES.
THIRD CL.
1515

113. Class E4 no. 32508 backs onto the one coach arrival from the south, to form a train for Lewes via Sheffield Park. The smoke from the C2X that had brought it in can be seen under the bridge. A Three Bridges bound push-pull set with gangway connection can be seen at the high-level, in December 1957. (P. Hay)

114. The last passenger train to Lewes was the 4.28 p.m. on 16th March 1958. The locomotive carrying the Wilted Bluebell headboard was class 4 no. 80154, appropriate as it was the last engine to have been built at Brighton Locomotive Works. (J. Scrace)

115. Usually two island platforms are used for up and down trains, but here the left hand one was used by Oxted line trains, whilst the one on the right was mainly for Three Bridges journeys. The trains, from left to right, as seen from the West Signal Box on 23rd June 1962 are the 1.9 p.m. from Victoria; the 1.45 p.m. from Tunbridge Wells West (headed by class 4 tank no. 80139) and the 2.27 p.m. to Three Bridges, prior to tail lamp changing. (J.H. Aston)

117. Looking west in 1963 from near the upper goods yard gates we see the goods shed with its single storey office and beyond it is the 1855 station house. All freight facilities were withdrawn from 10th April 1967, the shed being demolished in 1976. (C. Vigor)

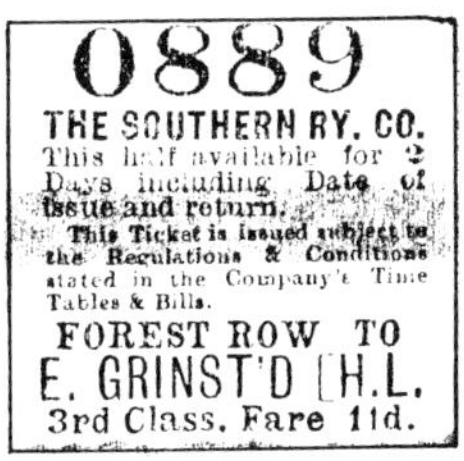

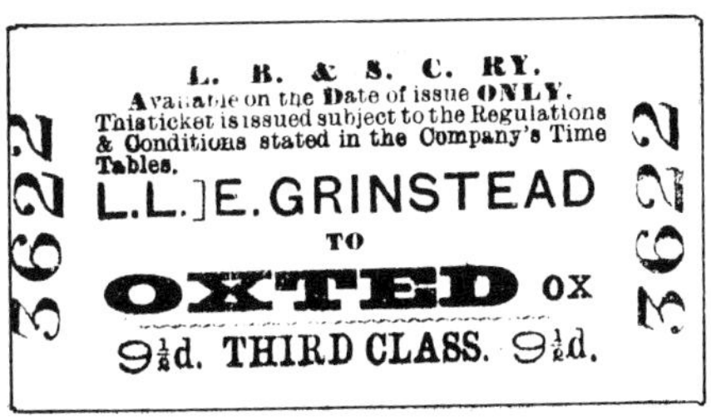

←

116. Another BR standard class 4 2–6–4 tank, this time passing East Box with a Victoria to Tunbridge Wells West train on 29th May 1963. The curved line on the extreme left of the picture connects the upper and lower yards. (J. Scrace)

118. After the closure of the Lewes line in 1958, the low level platforms were little used until the east-west service was withdrawn in 1967, when high level was closed. Here we see, in February 1970, a new footbridge under construction and demolition of the station starting. (R. Pook)

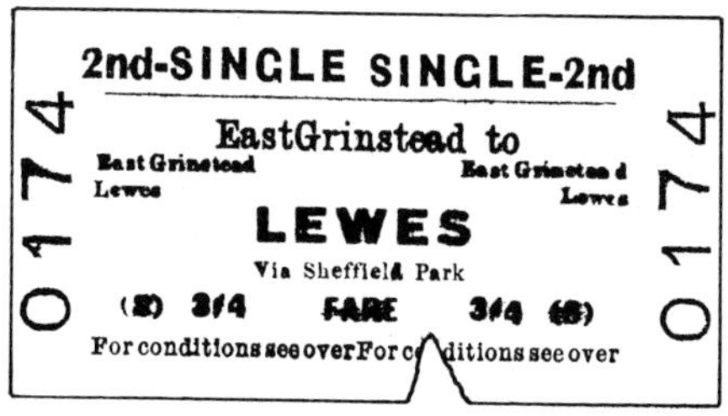

119. A rare visitor, on 7th April 1979, was this class 50 locomotive from the Western Region, on a RPPR Railtour. Only three early morning trains now use the platform on the right (no. 2). The lower signal arm is for shunting purposes – for example, when a locomotive is running round its train. There are now only two locomotive hauled trains each way on weekdays, all others being DEMUs. (J.A.M. Vaughan)

120. Although nothing remains of the previous station building, the South Box is still in use and most of the track in the former coal yard is in place. Might the latter one day become the northern terminus of the Bluebell Railway? This, the town's fourth station, is now a true branch line terminus and long may it remain. (T. Middlemass)

MP Middleton Press

Easebourne Lane, Midhurst, W Sussex. GU29 9AZ Tel: 01730 813169 Fax: 01730 812601

If books are not available from your local transport stockist, order direct with cheque, Visa or Mastercard, post free UK.

BRANCH LINES
Branch Line to Allhallows
Branch Line to Alton
Branch Lines around Ascot
Branch Line to Ashburton
Branch Lines around Bodmin
Branch Line to Bude
Branch Lines around Canterbury
Branch Lines around Chard & Yeovil
Branch Lines around Cromer
Branch Lines of East London
Branch Lines to Effingham Junction
Branch Lines around Exmouth
Branch Line to Fairford
Branch Lines around Gosport
Branch Line to Hawkhurst
Branch Line to Hayling
Branch Lines to Horsham
Branch Lines around Huntingdon
Branch Line to Kingswear
Branch Lines to Launceston & Princetown
Branch Lines to Longmoor
Branch Line to Looe
Branch Line to Lyme Regis
Branch Lines around March
Branch Lines around Midhurst
Branch Line to Minehead
Branch Line to Moretonhampstead
Branch Lines to Newport (IOW)
Branch Line to Padstow
Branch Lines around Plymouth
Branch Lines to Seaton and Sidmouth
Branch Line to Selsey
Branch Lines around Sheerness
Branch Line to Shrewsbury
Branch Line to Swanage *updated*
Branch Line to Tenterden
Branch Lines to Torrington
Branch Lines to Tunbridge Wells
Branch Line to Upwell
Branch Lines around Weymouth
Branch Lines around Wimborne
Branch Lines around Wisbech

NARROW GAUGE BRANCH LINES
Branch Line to Lynton
Branch Lines around Portmadoc 1923-46
Branch Lines around Porthmadog 1954-94
Branch Line to Southwold
Two-Foot Gauge Survivors
Romneyrail
Vivarais Narrow Gauge

SOUTH COAST RAILWAYS
Ashford to Dover
Bournemouth to Weymouth
Brighton to Eastbourne
Brighton to Worthing
Dover to Ramsgate
Eastbourne to Hastings
Hastings to Ashford
Portsmouth to Southampton
Southampton to Bournemouth
Worthing to Chichester

SOUTHERN MAIN LINES
Basingstoke to Salisbury
Bromley South to Rochester
Crawley to Littlehampton
Dartford to Sittingbourne
East Croydon to Three Bridges
Epsom to Horsham
Exeter to Barnstaple
Exeter to Tavistock
Faversham to Dover
London Bridge to East Croydon
Orpington to Tonbridge
Tonbridge to Hastings
Salisbury to Yeovil
Swanley to Ashford
Tavistock to Plymouth
Victoria to East Croydon
Waterloo to Windsor
Waterloo to Woking
Woking to Portsmouth
Woking to Southampton
Yeovil to Exeter

EASTERN MAIN LINES
Fenchurch Street to Barking
Ipswich to Saxmundham
Liverpool Street to Ilford

WESTERN MAIN LINES
Ealing to Slough
Paddington to Ealing

COUNTRY RAILWAY ROUTES
Andover to Southampton
Bath Green Park to Bristol
Bath to Evercreech Junction
Bournemouth to Evercreech Jn.
Cheltenham to Andover
Croydon to East Grinstead
Didcot to Winchester
East Kent Light Railway
Fareham to Salisbury
Frome to Bristol
Guildford to Redhill
Porthmadog to Blaenau
Reading to Basingstoke
Reading to Guildford
Redhill to Ashford
Salisbury to Westbury
Stratford upon Avon to Cheltenham
Strood to Paddock Wood
Taunton to Barnstaple
Wenford Bridge to Fowey
Westbury to Bath
Woking to Alton
Yeovil to Dorchester

GREAT RAILWAY ERAS
Ashford from Steam to Eurostar
Clapham Junction 50 years of change
Festiniog in the Fifties
Festiniog in the Sixties
Isle of Wight Lines 50 years of change
Railways to Victory 1944-46
SECR Centenary album
Talyllyn 50 years of change
Yeovil 50 years of change

LONDON SUBURBAN RAILWAYS
Caterham and Tattenham Corner
Charing Cross to Dartford
Clapham Jn. to Beckenham Jn.
East London Line
Finsbury Park to Alexandra Palace
Kingston and Hounslow Loops
Lewisham to Dartford
Lines around Wimbledon
London Bridge to Addiscombe
Mitcham Junction Lines
North London Line
South London Line
West Croydon to Epsom
West London Line
Willesden Junction to Richmond
Wimbledon to Epsom

STEAMING THROUGH
Steaming through Cornwall
Steaming through Kent
Steaming through West Hants
Steaming through West Sussex

TRAMWAY CLASSICS
Aldgate & Stepney Tramways
Barnet & Finchley Tramways
Bath Tramways
Bournemouth & Poole Tramways
Brighton's Tramways
Camberwell & W.Norwood Tramways
Clapham & Streatham Tramways
Dover's Tramways
East Ham & West Ham Tramways
Edgware and Willesden Tramways
Eltham & Woolwich Tramways
Embankment & Waterloo Tramways
Enfield & Wood Green Tramways
Exeter & Taunton Tramways
Gosport & Horndean Tramways
Greenwich & Dartford Tramways
Hammersmith & Hounslow Tramways
Hampstead & Highgate Tramways
Hastings Tramways
Holborn & Finsbury Tramways
Ilford & Barking Tramways
Kingston & Wimbledon Tramways
Lewisham & Catford Tramways
Liverpool Tramways 1. Eastern Routes
Liverpool Tramways 2. Southern Routes
Maidstone & Chatham Tramways
North Kent Tramways
Norwich Tramways
Portsmouth's Tramways
Reading Tramways
Seaton & Eastbourne Tramways
Shepherds Bush & Uxbridge Tramways
Southampton Tramways
Southend-on-sea Tramways
Southwark & Deptford Tramways
Stamford Hill Tramways
Twickenham & Kingston Tramways
Victoria & Lambeth Tramways
Waltham Cross & Edmonton Tramways
Walthamstow & Leyton Tramways
Wandsworth & Battersea Tramways

TROLLEYBUS CLASSICS
Croydon Trolleybuses
Bournemouth Trolleybuses
Hastings Trolleybuses
Maidstone Trolleybuses
Reading Trolleybuses
Woolwich & Dartford Trolleybuses

WATERWAY ALBUMS
Kent and East Sussex Waterways
London to Portsmouth Waterway
West Sussex Waterways

MILITARY BOOKS
Battle over Portsmouth
Battle over Sussex 1940
Blitz over Sussex 1941-42
Bombers over Sussex 1943-45
Bognor at War
Military Defence of West Sussex
Secret Sussex Resistance
Sussex Home Guard

OTHER RAILWAY BOOKS
Garraway Father & Son
Index to all Middleton Press stations
Industrial Railways of the South-East
South Eastern & Chatham Railways
London Chatham & Dover Railway
War on the Line (SR 1939-45)